Cambridge Elements ≡

Elements in Beckett Studies
edited by
Dirk Van Hulle
University of Oxford
Mark Nixon
University of Reading

SAMUEL BECKETT'S GEOLOGICAL IMAGINATION

Mark Byron
University of Sydney

CAMBRIDGE
UNIVERSITY PRESS

CAMBRIDGE
UNIVERSITY PRESS

University Printing House, Cambridge CB2 8BS, United Kingdom

One Liberty Plaza, 20th Floor, New York, NY 10006, USA

477 Williamstown Road, Port Melbourne, VIC 3207, Australia

314–321, 3rd Floor, Plot 3, Splendor Forum, Jasola District Centre,
New Delhi – 110025, India

79 Anson Road, #06–04/06, Singapore 079906

Cambridge University Press is part of the University of Cambridge.

It furthers the University's mission by disseminating knowledge in the pursuit of
education, learning, and research at the highest international levels of excellence.

www.cambridge.org
Information on this title: www.cambridge.org/9781108738965
DOI: 10.1017/9781108772457

First published 2020

A catalogue record for this publication is available from the British Library.

ISBN 978-1-108-73896-5 Paperback
ISSN 2632-0746 (online)
ISSN 2632-0738 (print)

Samuel Beckett's Geological Imagination

Elements in Beckett Studies

DOI: 10.1017/9781108772457
First published online: September 2020

Mark Byron
University of Sydney

Author for correspondence: Mark Byron, mark.byron@sydney.edu.au

Abstract: *Samuel Beckett's Geological Imagination* addresses the ubiquity of earthy objects in Beckett's prose, drama, and poetry, exploring how mineral and archaeological objects bear upon the themes, narrative locus, and sensibilities of Beckett's texts in surprisingly varied ways. By deploying figures of ruination and excavation with etymological self-awareness, Beckett's late prose narratives – *Company, Ill Seen Ill Said,* and *Worstward Ho* – comprise a late-career meditation on the stratigraphic layerings of language and memory over an extended writing career. These layers comprise an embodied record of writing in their allusions to literary history and to Beckett's own oeuvre.

Keywords: geology, archaeology, etymology, stone, intertextuality

ISBNs: 9781108738965 (PB), 9781108772457 (OC)
ISSNs: 2632-0746 (online), 2632-0738 (print)

Contents

Introduction

> Changed the stone that draws her when revisited alone. Or she who changes it when
> side by side. Now alone it leans. Backward or forward as the case may be. Is it to
> nature alone it owes its rough-hewn air? Or to some too human hand forced to desist?
> – *Ill Seen Ill Said*

In a story full of stones – fieldstone, megaliths, threshold stones, terrestrial planets, and satellites – *Ill Seen Ill Said* provides a grounding point for human agency and narrative subjectivity in the funerary stele ritually visited by the woman. This passage appears three-quarters of the way through the text, at which point the pull between the woman and the rocky landscape surrounding her hovel prompts questions of a more foundational kind regarding the human–stone relation at work in the narrative. On first sight these sentences seem to reflect upon the possibility and range of human agency as the protagonist is shaped by the narrating voice and observing eye, on the one hand, and as she approaches the condition of stone in her advancing moments of stasis, on the other. But a closer look at the prose suggests that agency is reversible, where stone becomes the actant – it 'draws her' – and human agency retreats – the 'too human hand forced to desist'. The line between natural and carved stone becomes fuzzy, and the magnetism between human and stone seems to blend their identities together: 'The stone draws her' – as though composing a character sketch or narrative outline. The passage also draws attention to the artifice of narrative composition in the dense assonance and alliteration of its final two sentences. These lines also sound a dim echo: the 'too human' of Friedrich Nietzsche's *Human, All Too Human: A Book for Free Spirits* (*Menschliches, Allzumenschliches: Ein Buch für freie Geister* [1878]) – his first work in the aphoristic style and one that seeks to invert the customary paradigm of rationality and animality.

Beckett's *geological imagination* probes the porous boundaries between human and mineral realms. Just as stone exerts its force on the construction of character, a lithic vocabulary draws attention to complex textual stratifications: layers of composition, the deployment of literary intertextuality and etymology, and the archaeology of memory undertaken by his narrators and by the author memorializing a substantial oeuvre. This geological imagination is evident throughout Beckett's career, but becomes fully articulated in the late prose texts of *Company*, *Ill Seen Ill Said*, and *Worstward Ho*, where a compulsive return to matters of the earth coexists with an intensely reflexive notion of the *matter* of literary production, in all its senses. This intimate relation between textual objects and textual substance fundamentally structures these late prose works, in the process grounding an archaeological method for reading them.

Bedrock

Geology and mineralogy is everywhere in Samuel Beckett's work, from Molloy's sucking stones and the clink of the stonecutters' chisels in *Watt*, to the piece of grit on the steppe in *Endgame* and Estragon's Tarpeian Rock in *Waiting for Godot*, to the standing stones of *Ill Seen Ill Said* and the terrain of 'rift' and 'vast' in *Worstward Ho*. Beckett's deployment of geological imagery bears a specific relation to the stratified nature of memory and textual production, evident in the various ways he reanimates his own biography in the service of fiction. As a child he would collect stones from the beach at Greystones during summer holidays and store them in tree branches at home (Knowlson, 1996, 29), and his tramping the countryside and mountains of County Dublin and Wicklow with his father or alone directly informs the imagery, topography, and narrative scene in several of his prose and dramatic texts. Beckett's engagement with the history of Ireland and its profound literary and linguistic heritage has received sustained critical attention, including recent historicist and postcolonial evaluations, but his focus extends beyond and beneath the history of human habitation of the land to the geological forces giving it shape and texture.

Several of Beckett's characters aspire to the condition of stone, and Beckett gestures towards this bodily geology in a letter to Mary Manning Howe of 22 May 1937 when he compares his own cardiac arrhythmia to the 'hardened chest' of his friend George Pelorson, a kind of 'cardiac calculus' immune to the foibles of his own soft organic condition (quoted in Dukes, 2016, 35). He writes to Cissie Sinclair of Jack B. Yeats and to Thomas McGreevy of Jean-Antoine Watteau as artists of the inorganic, whose figures are petrified or mineral (*LI* 536 and 540). Beckett's characters and narrators navigate the varieties of geology, excavation, ruined landscapes, and human habitations – and indeed the decayed location of the human body and mind and their records in speech and script. If they ultimately seek to return to the condition of stone – as the figure of the woman illustrates in *Ill Seen Ill Said* – not only do they find geology exerting its own force upon them, but they engage with a terrestrial zone in which vast systems of life abide, hidden from view, further complicating the relation with the inorganic.

Recent research into 'deep life' has discovered a massive subterranean biosphere at extreme depths and temperatures within the earth's crust, making up seventy percent of the earth's bacteria and *archaea*, single-celled microorganisms lacking nuclei called *prokaryotes* (see Deep Carbon Observatory). Contrary to notions of the subsurface earth functioning primarily as a repository for the end of life (the grave) or the absence of life (minerals and archaeological ruins), it is instead the place where most life is to be found, entirely separated from what goes on at the surface. This deep life resonates with allusions to such minerals as chalk and limestone in Beckett's work, which are composed of skeletal fragments of marine organisms such as corals and molluscs. These relations between the animate and the mineral, between life and non-life, underline the subtlety of Beckett's mineralogical metaphors and how they register the complicity between the dimensions of life and the inanimate. These metaphors regulate the relations between narrative subjects and objects, voice and inscription, motion and stasis, and the text surface and its archive: the fictionalized documents and revisions within specific narratives as well as Beckett's physical notebooks and other objects of his grey canon; the store of intertextual references including Beckett's own work; and the workings of memory in narrators and characters within and across his texts.

Styles of Interment

Beckett's geological imagination finds its full force in the texts of *Nohow On*, but these narratives demonstrate continuities with his oeuvre and illustrate his lifelong working methods. From at least as early as *Murphy* Beckett's prose narratives draw attention to themselves as constructed, mediated objects. This reflexive mode of writing is given expression in the presence of footnotes and addenda, breaks in the text surface, the lurking shadows of editors and scribes, and narrators breaking the 'fourth wall' to comment upon the conditions of writing or devising the text at issue, or to reflect upon (and often withdraw) specific narrative choices. Narrators contemplate the design of their worlds and the agency of their long-suffering subjects, and they often seek recourse in geological and archaeological images, allusions, and etymologies. *Company*, *Ill Seen Ill Said*, and *Worstward Ho* each raise the intensity of this narrative and textual reflexivity, and they demonstrate Beckett's intensive focus on matters of the earth – cromlechs, statuary, buried objects, geology and geomorphology, and especially the dense etymological textures that ground his language in geological metaphors and images. His narrators exercise their creative powers of imagination by raising (and withdrawing) aspects of character, where the potential capacity for consciousness in protean narrative subjects invokes questions of narrative agency and the possibilities of writing in the first instance.

Despite such continuities, the three late narratives of *Nohow On* embody a shift in the way textual awareness and geological tropes relate to one another: they become twinned aspects of a subtle archaeological project in which the stratigraphy of Beckett's oeuvre, and the literary tradition with which it engages, reveals itself in the language and imagery of these late texts. As narrators raise effigies of character, this verbal statuary casts a critical reflection upon the status of the textual object: a porous surface constructed on the layers of deep time, manifested in literary reference to Beckett's own texts and to specific aspects of the literary tradition, particularly Romantic poetry. The question of agency imbued in the creation of character – when and how do these effigies attain consciousness? can they approach the condition of stone? – and the potential agency of the lithic objects with which they interact transforms from a theoretical concern to a mode of reflection on the text object itself. Each of *Company, Ill Seen Ill Said*, and *Worstward Ho* bears metafictional residues, but in crossing between narrative reflexivity and a contemplation of textual materiality – the surfaces on which texts are inscribed and their capacity for disintegration and preservation – these narratives become archaeological objects in their own right. As the workings of memory produce an archaeology of the mind – Beckett's debt to psychology and to Freud in particular – textual memory is embodied in the materiality of narrative and the constitution of the words and images that bind them together: literary reference, etymology, and the bare fact of inscription on paper and stone.

Company turns on the production of narrative subjects – who may be figments or confected objects given temporary animation – in the act of narrating remembered episodes from earlier texts, which themselves manifest a provenance in Beckett's biography. This archaeology of memory anchors itself in images of geology, Neolithic structures, and geomorphology, where the etymology of key words and intertextual reference circle back to earthy matters. The affinity between the workings of the narrative mind and matters of geology in *Company* becomes the substance or fabric of the text in *Ill Seen Ill Said*. The narrative mise en scène is dominated by the hovel with its flagstone, the 'zone of stones', the 'Twelve' – a Neolithic standing stone circle – and the headstone of a burial site. But the old woman is its epicentre, closely observed by the narrator who sees her approach the condition of stone. Etymology and literary reference turn on geological concepts and imagery, as though the narrator attempts to bridge the subjectivity retained by the woman with the narrative object she approaches but does not quite become. *Worstward Ho* turns the geological imagination a degree further, fusing the production of text material with the language of geomorphology. As character is diminished into three 'shades', the creation and decreation of these narrative objects impel an intensive geological vocabulary. The diminishment of character into partially realized narrative objects, set within a landscape grounded in geological etymologies, culminates in the image of pinpricks in a page, where the ground of composition is not the landscape of realist narrative but the projection of images in a camera obscura, returning the reader to Beckett's early ambition to puncture the veil of language to reveal the nothingness behind.

The four sections of this Element trace out the evolution of Beckett's geological imagination. The first section provides an overview across numerous dramatic works, novels and short prose, as well as the occasional poem, to demonstrate the consistency with which Beckett draws on his geological fund. There is a surprising richness in these themes and images, and while they do vary in their effects – the earlier prose works draw on the topography of Wicklow where the later prose tends to engage in more abstract themes of desolation or confinement – the aim is to provide a broad context for the sections to follow rather than to engage in extended analysis. This having been said, the continuities with the three sections that follow are clear – each dwells on a single text of *Nohow On* – especially when considered in relation to such themes as posthumanism, theories of the object, textual genesis, and the material or archival turn in Modernism Studies.

Field Objects

Beckett's late prose engages geological images and concepts in ways that are grounded in the constitution of the text itself: etymology evident in deliberate word choices, literary allusion, and the production of reflexive narratives with their own material bases in the fictionalized act of writing. These strategies suggest strong affinities with recent theoretical and analytic work on materialism, objects, and thinghood. Geological and archaeological objects invite consideration of their provenance as well as their relation to the narrative and its various subjects. They also invite consideration with regard to the posthumanist development of New Materialism or Object-Oriented Ontology: a field (or fields) in which human agency does not comprise a central or even a peripheral concern, but instead the agency of things prevails, especially non-living objects. This philosophical development finds its dominant expression in literary studies and gender studies (Grusin, 2015; Braidotti, 2013; Bogost, 2012; Harmon, 2002) as well as political science (Bennett, 2010; Coole and Frost, 2010), and informs recent work in Beckett Studies: in Jonathan Boulter's *Posthuman Space in Samuel Beckett's Shorter Prose* (2019), Derval Tubridy's *Samuel Beckett and the Language of Subjectivity* (2018), Julie Bates's *Beckett's Art of Salvage: Writing and Material Imagination, 1932–1987* (2017), Steven Connor's *Beckett, Modernism, and the Material Imagination* (2014), and in shorter studies by Jean-Michel Rabaté (2016) and Alexander Price (2014), among others.

Boulter calls *Company, Ill Seen Ill Said*, and *Worstward Ho* 'fables of posthuman space', suggesting how New Materialism can inform the ways narrative space and physical space can be thought of as mutually constitutive, opening the way for the study of geology and archaeology in Beckett's late prose buttressed by these theoretical and analytic advances. Archaeology, a field that has the study of inanimate objects of human fabrication at its core, has also turned to questions of the agency of objects (Olsen, 2010; Olsen, Chanks, Webmoor, and Witmore, 2012). Jeffrey Jeremy Cohen brings into focus the large scale of geologic time and the lithic presence in literature (with an emphasis on medieval literature) in *Stone: An Ecology of the Inhuman* (2015). By placing the non-human, and even the non-animate, at the centre of questions of agency, this broad field of inquiry displaces the anthropocentric reflex in thinking about place, space, and the existence of things.

The word *thing* itself embeds temporal processes – deriving from the Old English and Old Norse *þing* ('assembly, meeting') and the Proto-Indo-European root **tenk-* ('stretch of time'). Although its meaning later changed to 'entity' or 'matter', the transactional implications embedded in the term *thing* have become something of a focal point in contemporary theory and are being read productively in modern literary representations of things, particularly in Beckett's texts. As Olsen notes: 'Things are not just traces or residues of absent presents; they are effectively engaged in assembling and hybridizing periods and epochs' (Olsen, 2010, 108). Beckett's insistent foregrounding of objects and their agency in narrative, precariously balanced with intensely self-aware (and often fragmented or disintegrating) narrative agents, plays out precisely this kind of thinking about the imposition of human agency upon a world formed by virtue of its force. But more than this, Beckett's objects – and none more so than his mineralogical objects such as the standing stones of *Ill Seen Ill Said* – begin to push back, asserting an agency of their own: agency separate from the human and in several respects shaping and even constituting the latter in a reversal of the anthropocentric scene.

Each of these recent directions in literary studies bears obvious connections to Beckett's geological imagination. But Beckett's narrators and dramatic interlocutors also deal in themes such as the possibility of consciousness, the contemplation of free agency and the fear of compulsion, the zone of dreams and the unconscious and its intersections with conscious life, and the workings of memory and trauma – mental, emotional, and physical. How do these dimensions of Beckett's texts engage with the geological?

Themes of mind and consciousness find expression in geological images and tropes in a range of texts across Beckett's career – as will be elaborated in the next section – but the specific terms of reflexivity in evidence in the texts of *Nohow On* introduce new methods for thinking through geology and consciousness. Extended Mind theory, elaborated by Andy Clark and David Chalmers in 1998, proposes that objects in the world can be considered as part of the mind's apparatus. The processes of consciousness operate as a coupled system, where external objects extend the mind into the world as long as they function with similar purpose to 'internal' faculties of the mind. Beckett's prominent use of prosthetic devices in his fiction and drama – Malone's notebooks and pencil, wheelchairs in *Endgame* and *Rough for Theatre I*, bicycles, prods, and even other characters – all suggest the notion of bodily and cognitive extension as a lifelong preoccupation. Yet in the later prose works the deeply reflexive nature of narration, and its capacity to register itself and the narrative world it describes on a singular plane of immanence, animates some of these external objects in fundamental ways.

Text Mining

The rise of digital methods in literary studies has produced new ways of thinking about how literary content relates to the wider discursive formations of literature. Franco Moretti's model of distant reading has proved to be influential in thinking about larger structures of literary production and consumption, especially when trained upon long historical periods, diverse geographic and national contexts, and very large corpora of printed material. The Beckett Digital Manuscript Project is the leading application of digital methods to Beckett's work. In this case the focus rests upon manuscript and prepublication material rather than a published corpus, and although the BDMP offers new ways of seeing and understanding the larger contours of Beckett's writing career – the contents and annotative dimension of his personal library, for example – some of the most exciting and productive opportunities afforded by the project pertain to close reading of texts and close attention to their composition histories. In this sense Beckett's profile in the digital age accords closely with metaphors of mining, where texts, manuscripts, letters, and other materials are plumbed for their contents and their contexts, to explore how they combine into a larger intellectual and imaginative system. Such scholarly methods stimulate metaphors of geological stratification by squaring specific texts with their genetic archives. This study reads Beckett's late prose narratives as material expressions of his geological imagination, where attention to detailed matters of philology, etymology, stylistic change, and the progressive 'vaguening' of literary reference – including to his own earlier texts – shows how geological themes and images govern the relations of narrative subjects and objects, memory and inscription, bare life, and the agency of things.

Text mining takes two dominant forms in this study: firstly, a focus on the origin and provenance of particular words reveals a vocabulary of the 'underground', where words occurring at pivotal points in the texts of *Nohow On* turn on geological or terranean points of origin; secondly, the texts of *Nohow On* are mined with attention to how they engage in literary reference, as well as their strategic citation of Beckett's earlier works. Beckett's processes of allusion are famously vague, prone to descriptions of erosion, sedimentation, fossilization, and other metaphors implicated in matters of mining and archaeology. The question of how close reading and 'deep' etymological analysis might intersect with digital methods is worth careful consideration.

Beckett Studies has led the so-called 'documentary turn' in Modernism Studies, due in no small part to James Knowlson's 1996 biography *Damned to Fame*, which provided an enormous range of information concerning Beckett's working methods, as well as the condition and status of his pre-publication archive. Genetic studies of a number of texts (Krance, 1993; Krance, 1996; Hisgen and van der Weel, 1998; O'Reilly, 2001) have demonstrated how these working methods actively constitute the way matters of vocabulary, self-citation, and intertextual references operate at or partially beneath the surface of the text. The publication of Beckett's four-volume *Selected Letters* and numerous editions of draft stories, early notebooks, and caches of working notes has opened the archive to a greater extent and to a wider field of scholarship and readership than is the case with almost any other author. This generational shift in Beckett Studies has placed renewed emphasis on the status of the so-called 'grey canon'. Metaphors of mining, sifting, literary and documentary strata, examination of tailings, deciphering worn archaeological shards, and interpreting the presence of 'fossils' often arise when describing the ways in which scholarship and editorial labour have been enriched by access to these resources. There is not sufficient space in the present study to elaborate all the methodological and conceptual enrichments of the documentary turn in Beckett Studies. But a critical evaluation of the ways geological and lithic concepts are deployed in Beckett's texts suggests rich potential avenues for future research in their resonances with current scholarly practices and theoretical formations.

The Scottish sculptor Andy Goldworthy's observation, 'A stone is ingrained with geological and historical memories' (quoted in Long, 2016, 139), captures the essence of Beckett's geological imagination from the viewpoint of an artistic practitioner working with stone and discovering a rich inanimate life. The stone has memories: it is an extension of the sculptor's arm and chisel. Stone informs the narrator's apprehension of landscape, distributed identity, and history. Beckett's stones appear in fields, unmediated, or as standing stones that register the depth of human history. They draw in his protagonists, whether by forces of narrative magnetism or gravity, and they present an inanimate face to the visage of the observer. His stones address the reader too, enjoining us to hear the echoes and resonances from history and literature: the Tarpeian Rock, a cliff located on the Capitoline Hill in Rome; the Rock of Peter upon which the Christian Church was founded; the gravestones (historical and anonymous) in the graveyards of Christendom and the fields of pagany; the Colossi of Memnon, guardians of the tomb of Amenhotep III in Thebes; and even the remnant feet of Ozymandias, jutting out from the desert of bare narrative landscape to suggest hidden antiquities beneath the surface. Beckett's protagonists imagine themselves as stone, engineer ways of measuring their identities with them, or find them useful (or painful) instruments of violence. There is little sculpting of stone in Beckett's texts, but the excavatory spirit arises in the presence of mud or in the suggestion of literary quotation. Texts are given the status of ground as much as the earthworks Beckett's narrators and characters discover, and the act of narration often gives rise to fantasias of epigraphy – such as the figure in *Molloy* gazing upon the landscape 'as if to engrave the landmarks on his memory' (*MY* 6) – as though inscribing one's name in stone secures otherwise intangible aspects of character and identity. Beckett's stones are nearly everywhere, worked by narration as often as by prior hands, passed down through landscapes, history, and literature, and always measuring the bodies and minds of his own people.

1 'Saxa Loquuntur!'

> Imagine that an explorer arrives in a little-known region where his interest is aroused by an expanse of ruins, with remains of walls, fragments of columns, and tablets with half-effaced and unreadable inscriptions. He may content himself with inspecting what lies exposed to view, with questioning the inhabitants – perhaps semi-barbaric people – who live in the vicinity, about what tradition tells them of the history and meaning of these archaeological remains, and with noting down what they tell him – and he may then proceed on his journey. But he may act differently. He may have brought picks, shovels and spades with him, and he may set the inhabitants to work with these implements. Together with them he may start upon the ruins, clear away the rubbish, and, beginning from the visible remains, uncover what is buried. If his work is crowned with success, the discoveries are self-explanatory; the ruined walls are part of the ramparts of a palace or a treasure-house; the fragments of columns can be filled out into a temple; the numerous inscriptions, which, by good luck, may be bilingual, reveal an alphabet and a language, and, when they have been deciphered and translated, yield undreamed-of information about the events of the remote past, to commemorate which the monuments were built. *Saxa loquuntur.*
>
> (Freud, 1962, 189; quoted in Hake, 1993, 148)

Sigmund Freud published 'The Aetiology of Hysteria' in 1896, in the twilight of a century that had seen profound developments in archaeology: the method of stratigraphy and its illumination of the earth's deep time; scientific dating of exhumed objects; and transformative excavations such as Heinrich Schliemann's at Troy from 1871 and Mycenae in 1876, and Arthur Evans's Minoan discoveries at Knossus, Crete, from 1900. Freud deploys archaeological metaphors for the depths of the human mind, particularly the unconscious, shaped by the earliest experiences and buried beneath the regular workings of memory. This association of rock, masonry, excavation, epigraphy, and deep time with the gradual revelation of the self by expert use of the tools of exhumation – the patient as quarry – bore profound effects on the discipline of psychoanalysis in which Beckett became intimately knowledgeable at the time of his own analysis with Walter Bion at the Tavistock Clinic in 1934–5. Freud concludes his excavatory parable with the Latinized term for epigraphy or the study of ancient inscriptions (O'Donoghue, 2019, 42), but he leaves open the possibility that the stones speak in themselves as much as through any inscription they might bear. This phrase was likely taken from the burial plaque of Vienna's pre-eminent architect, Friedrich Schmidt (1825–91), who named the city's Rathaus *Saxa loquuntur* and adopted the phrase as his personal motto. Freud neatly brings together a series of themes and images in his parable of the human mind as a site of living excavation, each of which finds expression in Beckett's texts: ruins, earth, stones, buried objects, inscriptions, gravestones, and their (often partial) visibility and intelligibility. The sense of human consciousness as an ontogenetic process – one retrospectively understood across its various stages of development – is tempered by the deep histories of the human species, where, for example, breaking ground in tillage is fundamental for sedentary society. Evidence for such deep histories is found in the earth, in fields cleared of rock and trees, and in the stone monuments left behind. There is symmetry in Beckett turning an earthy vocabulary to identify and describe the human mind, as well as remnant inscriptions left behind, not least in those final epitaphs on the funeral *stelae* littering his texts.

As Freud's extended metaphor suggests, imagery concerned with archaeology, digging, and tilling the earth bears a provocative analogy to the excavations of the human mind, but embodied as textual matter it also suggests particular metatextual and hermeneutic themes. It draws attention to textual layers in the processes of composition, degrees of citation and allusion, and the relation of a text to a writer's oeuvre. It invokes specific practices of analytic excavation, whether close reading, etymological analysis, or the indexing of intertextual and reflexive modes of reference. An archaeological dig will be conducted on the basis of specific location choices in the knowledge that potentially significant finds may remain out of reach. Spatial metaphors of breadth and depth – the topographical range of the excavation as well as its penetration through various stratigraphic layers – also bear upon temporal metaphors: the accretive understanding of an excavation site and the objects it reveals unfold over an excavation's history, even over the course of centuries in the case of Pompeii and the Neolithic barrows of Wiltshire.

In analogous ways, the overview of Beckett's geological investigations in this section trains attention upon how Beckett deploys his geological imagination across his career up to the texts of *Nohow On*, from realist depictions of geology and stone structures in *More Pricks Than Kicks* to increasingly abstracted uses of stone architecture and recycled pathways in the *Fizzles* and other late prose texts. This usage is suggestive of how archaeology and geology become expressions of language and memory and are themselves expressive of narrative immanence: the folding of textual production and the fictional world into each other. These examples can be arranged into a loose typology: stones, tillage, archaeology, masonry, and what Beckett called 'auto-speliology': the psychological excavations of the human mind, a notion that extends to how Beckett recycles archaisms and makes allusion to both his literary predecessors and to his own earlier works.

Abode of Stones

Beckett's abundant use of lithic imagery comprises an important part of his aesthetic: from the geological textures of place, to the handling of stones as weapons, memory devices, or, in the final event, as markers of a burial or memorial to the deceased. Stone serves as a conceit for the processes of composition, from the dredging of creative material from the unconscious, to its commitment to manuscript, and finally to its embodiment in texts that may be translated, edited, and subject to hermeneutic processes by readers. Stone is often deployed in ambivalent ways, in order to cause injury or to signify effacement, or to provide diversions from narrative progress.

The ancient practice of stone stacking is culturally ubiquitous across most of the world, a synecdoche for a longstanding inhabitation of the land, or even for the notion of prehistory itself. Such uses include markers for navigation and astronomy (the Arctic / Inuit *Inuksuk* or the Arabic *Rujm*), and the representation of human form (the Inuit *Inunnguak* or the Italian alpine *ometto*), of divinities (the Korean *Seonangdang*), or of architectural structures ('pagoda' stone stacks in Japanese and Korean Buddhist temple grounds). Stone stacks may also serve as altars in their own right such as the Mongolian *ovoo*, the Polynesian *ahu*, and the Norse *hörgr*, and are often located within larger stone structures such as the Hawai'ian *heiau*, the Polynesian *marae*, and the Maori *tohunga*. Beckett's early familiarity with the Neolithic and Bronze Age stone structures in the Wicklow Mountains, such as cairns, *tumuli*, *cromlechs*, Ogham stones, *kistvaens*, and *dolmens*, provided him with a rich symbolic reservoir for his fiction. These structures were sites for physical burial or bore memorial functions, giving Beckett ancient analogues for the gravestones and cemeteries that arise throughout his fiction: 'While these stones might have functioned as mythological gravestones, they were also entwined with the living – for there was a belief that druids were able to turn living humans into stone' (Dukes, 2016, 29; see also Bonwick, 1986). The shape of cairns also provided Beckett with ancient analogues for *clocháns* or beehive huts sprinkled in *All Strange Away* and elsewhere: monastic buildings dating from the seventh and eighth centuries and found in the southwest of Ireland, especially on the Dingle Peninsula and Skellig Michael in County Kerry.

Beckett's narrators and characters revel in the use of individual stones, whether arranged in emulation of Neolithic cairns or used as portable objects. Lady McCann strikes Watt with a stone when observing his 'funambulistic stagger' on the road (*W* 24), inducing a flow of blood staunched with his 'little red sudarium' as well as a phase of spiritual ecstasy or concussion (25–8). The *sudarium*, originally a face cloth in Roman times, was adapted for Christian liturgical use – the most famous examples being the Shroud of Turin, the Veil of Veronica, and the Sudarium of Oviedo, all ἀχειροποίητα (*acheiropoieta*) or images of Christ's face not made by human hands. That the narrator, and by implication Watt himself, would refer to Watt's kerchief in such terms is telling: on his train journey preceding his bruising walk Watt engaged in theological discussion with a fellow passenger Dum Spiro (*dum spiro, spero* – 'whilst I breathe, I hope'); and the mathematical basis of the angelic choir's lyrics bears associations with the ancient and complex Catholic tradition of *computus*, the calculation of Easter, the most important date in the Roman calendar (see Mosshammer, 2008). Watt also stands in for Saint Stephen, the first Christian martyr and patron saint of stonemasons, who was stoned to death (Acts 7:54–60).

Stones perform manifold functions in both the Old and New Testaments of the Bible: Jacob's dream of the ladder to heaven as he slept with stones for a pillow, which he then assembled into a pillar to mark Bethel, the place of God's covenant (Genesis 28:11–22); the twelve stones representing the Twelve Tribes of Israel taken into the River Jordan (Joshua 4:2–9, 20–4); 'A time to cast away stones, and a time to gather stones together' (Ecclesiastes 3:5); Peter as the rock upon which the Church is built (Matthew 16:18); the stone at the entrance of the tomb of Lazarus (John 11:38–44); and the displaced tombstone upon the resurrection of Christ (Luke 24:2). Stones also performed basic ceremonial and talismanic functions in classical Greece: the *omphalos* stone at Delphi, a white stone according to Pausanius and Pindar, 'functions as a hierophany, that is, a fixed point that opposes the "formless," homogeneous, amorphous expanse that characterizes profane space'; and roadside stones or *hermai* (ἑρμαῖ, sculpted heads on squared blocks) offered protection against 'the loneliness of the roads, the fearsomeness of the night, and stood for the protection of the traveller, house and field' (Rodriguez, 2004, 113 and 111, quoting Eliade, 1996, 235 and 231).

Watt could have done with an effective *herma*. Characters in other prose and dramatic texts make use of stones as portable devices: the narrator of 'The Calmative' carries a 'friendly stone' out of habit rather than protection (*TC* 33); the narrator of 'The Expelled' knocks on a cab door with a stone from his pocket (*EX* 11); in *Rough for Radio II* Fox narrates his life 'living dead in the stones', 'all stones all sides' (*ATF* 63, 62); in *Cascando* Voice tells of Woburn's face 'in the stones' as he scrambles his way from the boreen, 'face in the mud' (*ATF* 86), to the 'bare dunes' and the cave on the beach (87); and the woman's voice in *Eh Joe* '[s]coops a little cup for her face in the stones', kisses, and then fondles them as she narrates her death 'near the Rock' on the beach (*ATF* 118–19). Malone proposes his third story 'about a thing, a stone probably' (*MD* 6). His first story has Saposcat hide his books under a stone (19), and he expresses pity for 'little portable things in wood and stone' he salvages and keeps in his pocket until he wearies of them and either buries them or throws them into the sea (76). He also falls asleep with a stone in his hand (76). The Unnamable seeks to extend his ontological reach by contemplating his manoeuvring a stick or releasing, 'at the right moment, a stone, stones' into the gloom that suffuses his 'kingdom' (*U* 76). Elsewhere he imagines himself in Promethean visage 'lashed to a rock, in the midst of silence' (129–30). Perhaps the most memorable episode in which stones appear is Molloy's legendary system of sucking stones: 'They were pebbles but I call them stones' (*MY* 69). At first mentioned in the singular – checking his pockets '[m]y sucking stone in particular was no longer there. But sucking stones abound on our beaches, when you know where to look for them' (43) – Molloy gathers 'a considerable store' and distributes 'say sixteen stones' between the four pockets of his trousers and greatcoat (69). He concludes his attempt to solve the problem of coincidentally sucking the same four stones as they circulate between his pockets by 'sitting on the shore, before the sea, the sixteen stones spread out before my eyes' (71). That is, the stones (or pebbles) confound his combinatorial faculties and by extension his capacity for sequential narrative. Instead he seeks solace in the granulated form of sand – another recurring geological trope in Beckett's work – into which his consciousness is more readily distributed, and from which the narrative can proceed in any number of directions.

Matters of scale and mobility enter into Beckett's mineralogical images, where at one end of the scale sand, grit, and mud obviate the mid-sized objecthood embodied by stones and rocks, and at the other end, geological formations such as rocky landscapes, beaches, and cliffs exert a subtle pressure on narrators and characters, positioned at the scale of the sublime yet rarely bearing such affective force. Taking Molloy's sucking stones as an example of mid-sized objecthood (and stone-as-tool) and his defeat on the beach 'crushing handfuls of sand' (71), his narrative opens observing A and C moving across the landscape – the Wicklow Mountains presented in the language of the sublime – and his ascent to a rocky crest: 'I was perched higher than the road's highest point and flattened what is more against a rock of the same colour as myself, that is grey' (6–7). Molloy's shift of scale from sand to stones to rocky outcrops comprises a geological register that indexes significance in the narrative, from utter triviality and abjection through to the mysteries of spiritual contemplation found in Moran's observation of his bees at the novel's conclusion. Beckett's negotiations with Gnosticism via E. M. Cioran and Schopenhauer is well known (Wimbush, 2016, 11), particularly its doctrine that the material world is a creation of a malevolent demiurge to be endured and transcended. The geological register established in *Molloy* and elsewhere provides a compelling way of thinking through this kind of antipathy towards the world, not necessarily to overturn it, but to make it a lived experience complete with pain, mystification, disgust, and even odd moments of satisfaction.

Beckett's characters and narrators occasionally engage in geological imagery on a planetary scale, for example when Krapp speaks of 'this old muckball' (*K* 10). In *How It Is* mud replaces stone as an organic medium of inscription, and thus becomes basic to textual production, precarious and always potentially under erasure. Malone speaks of 'the times when I go liquid and become like mud' (*MD* 51). The woman's voice in *Eh Joe* foretells his death – 'Mud thou art' (*ATF* 117) – a variation on the English Burial Service formula taken from the King James Bible: 'for dust thou art, and unto dust shalt thou return' (Genesis 3:19). Manuscript A of *Worstward Ho* also makes reference to mud and iron in sentences omitted from later typescripts and the published text: 'Nothing for it in the mud but get up & stand. The bones. The ground or floor whatever it is hard as iron' (quoted in van der Weel, 1998, 21). Local geological zones also figure prominently in several of Beckett's plays. The thirty-nine-year-old Krapp recalls his epiphany at the end of the Dun Loghaire jetty during a storm, where the elements of atmosphere, water, and geology come together in the 'great granite rocks the foam flying up in the light of the lighthouse' (*K* 9). Geological depth takes priority over landscape in *Waiting for Godot*, where 'Lucky's "abode of stones" refers to geological upheavals and his speech invokes geological time over historical or human time' (Keatinge, 2007, 324). The recurrent image of the shingle appears in Beckett's poem 'Dieppe' – 'encore le dernier reflux / le galet mort', 'against the last ebb / the dead shingle' (*SP* 46) – and it produces the auditory ground in *Embers* as Henry sits, stands, and has his boots crunch on the strand (*ATF* 35–47). Malone recalls his sojourn to the sea with its islands and peninsulas and caves, 'crouched on the sand and in the lee of the rocks with the smell of the seaweed and the wet rock and the howling of the wind the waves whipping me with foam or sighing on the beach softly clawing the shingle' (*MD* 53). Malone's recollected images recall those of Molloy, who varied his time between crawl[ing] into some hole somewhere' and his time on the beach – 'In the sand I was in my element' (*MY* 68) – sourcing his sucking stones. The two ashbins in *Endgame* are lined with sand, providing a neat physical analogy to Hamm's melodramatic statement, 'Nature has forgotten us', and Clov's reply, 'There's no more nature' (*E* 10). This littoral zone is put to work by Beckett's characters and narrators as an expectant geography, where the paradox of a large entity (the strand) comprised of minute particles (sand) enables epiphanies, modes of circumspection, practical systems of bodily activity, and other changes of state.

Earth and stone also merge with the physical features or psychic condition of numerous characters. Murphy considers his diminishing sense of agency in terms of dispersed earthen particles: '[t]he freedom of indifference, the indifference of freedom, the will dust in the dust of its object, the act a handful of sand let fall' (67). When the Unnamable attempts to divest himself of such personae as Worm and Mahood, he dreams of a time when 'upon us all the silence will fall again, and settle, like dust of [*sic*] sand, on the arena, after the massacres' (*U* 92), uniting images of Roman gladiatorial games (and the architectural monuments in which they took place) and the customary retreat of Beckett's characters into the void of silence and darkness. Elsewhere the Unnamable laments the way time fails to pass but accretes into suffocating dunes: 'why it buries you grain by grain neither dead nor alive, with no memory of anything, no hope of anything, no knowledge of anything, no history and no prospects, buried under the seconds, saying any old thing, your mouth full of sand' (107). Clov describes himself as a smithereen (*E* 11) – a splinter from a larger object, from the Irish word *smidiríní* ('small fragment') – from which Hamm extrapolates Clov's condition in his final years: 'You'll be sitting there, a speck in the void [. . .] like a little bit of grit in the middle of the steppe' (*E* 23–4). Hamm's florid imagery situates the human subject between two poles of the perceptible geological scale: the undifferentiated fragment – grit derives from the Old English *greot* (earth, sand) and speck from the Old English *specca* (spot, stain) – and the vast dimensions of the sublime in the 'void' and the grasslands of the Eurasian steppe (the geographical source of Proto-Indo-European and its descendant languages). Krapp counterpoints the global 'muck-ball' with his own diminutive status: his thirty-nine-year-old self 'separating the grain from the husks' that his later listening self surmises to be 'those things worth having when all the dust has – when all *my* dust has settled' (*K* 5). The figure of *Lessness* is situated in, and blends with, a bare vista of sand 'ash grey' containing the 'true refuge' of 'scattered ruins' (*TFN* 129); and in the seventh *Fizzle*, 'For to end yet again', the figure is located in 'grey sand as far as the eye can see long desert to begin', where the sand is 'pale as dust' beneath a sky equally an 'ocean of dust' (*TFN* 151). The language of these later narratives, especially the intensive phrasal repetition of *Lessness*, becomes cognate with the undifferentiated landscapes they describe.

Imagination Dead Imagine reverses this scalar geological image, where instead two human figures inside the rotunda take on the characteristics of stone – '[s]weat and mirror notwithstanding they might well pass for inanimate' (*TFN* 89) – and their abode is reduced in the vast empty space to 'that white speck lost in the whiteness' (89). This figuration of human-as-stone threads through Beckett's texts – culminating in *Ill Seen Ill Said* – such as when Malone provides Macmann with a Belacqua-like profile: 'he as rather of the earth earthy and ill-fitted for pure reason [. . .] a good half of his existence must have been spent in a motionlessness akin to that of stone' (*MD* 71). When applied to human figures, Beckett's geological images move between the minuscule ('smithereen') and the monumental (the 'Memnon pose' in *Malone Dies*, *The Unnamable*, and *Ill Seen Ill Said*). In each example human agency recedes into mineralogical muteness, opening the way for stone and rocks to take on their own agency in the texts of *Nohow On*.

Till Now

Straddling the particulate dimension of soil, sand, and dust, on one hand, and monumental statuary and planetary geology, on the other, is the human scale of agriculture. The transition from hunting and gathering to sedentary agrarian social organization in various locations across the globe – the so-called Neolithic Revolution – gave rise to more complex social organization as well as the earliest forms of urbanization. This order of things is reflected in the genres of classical poetry, where the composition of georgic poetry (from γεωργικά, 'agriculture') preceded didactic and epic poetry, serving as proof of proficiency before the poet attempted the higher genres. Beckett's predilection for agricultural terminology also manifests in the early stages of his writing career in *More Pricks Than Kicks*. As Belacqua burns his toast in 'Dante and the

Lobster' he contemplates the spots on the moon after Dante and Beatrice in Canto 2 of *Paradiso*, where, situated in the first heaven, Beatrice explains how visual perception and reason are insufficient to metaphysical understanding: 'For the tiller of the field the thing was simple, he had it from his mother. The spots were Cain with his truss of thorns, dispossessed, cursed from the earth, fugitive and vagabond' (*MP* 5). The tiller is the man of agriculture looking at the night sky, discerning Cain with his visual stigma and a lifetime of labour as a result of his killing his brother, the shepherd Abel. But Cain is the 'tiller of soil' in Genesis 4:2. Belacqua's 'mix-up' entails a famous crux in Dante's poem, where Beatrice refutes Dante's earlier physical theory of the moon's spots in the *Convivio* – that of denser and rarer matter diffusing light in variant ways. As Belacqua fails to understand the lesson in divine wisdom he also puts aside Beatrice's exegesis, thus siding with the tiller and the clan of Cain.

In 'Fingal' Belacqua and Winnie visit Feltrim Hill to observe a 'land of sanctuary'. Winnie replies: 'I see nothing but three acres and cows. You can't have Cincinnatus without a furrow' (*MP* 19). She rebukes Belacqua's naïve pastoralism in her reference to Lucius Quintius Cincinnatus, a farmer of the early Roman republic persuaded out of retirement to lead Rome in a successful battle against the neighbouring Aequi. Cincinnatus relinquished dictatorial power and returned to his farm following his victory, in a gesture of civic virtue or *fides* (de Wilde, 2012, 563–4). Winnie's reference yokes together civic virtue with agrarian cultivation – a reversal of the association of tillage with Cain, and thus stigma and sin. As they approach the Portrane Lunatic Asylum, with two Martello towers, a water tower, and a round tower in view, '[t]hey followed the grass margin of a ploughed field till they came to where a bicycle was lying, half hidden in the rank grass' (20). This scene combines agriculture and modern technology – modern bicycle manufacture having only begun in the 1890s (see Byron, 2014) – but crucially intermediated by the uncultivated ground of 'rank grass'. This intrusion of uncultivated land collapses the sense of historical chronology from agriculture to industry, returning the scene to one of playful anachronism: 'Belacqua could see the man scraping away at his furrow and felt a sudden longing to be down there in the clay, lending a hand' (21). Belacqua and Winnie are occupied with walls, fields, and ruins – knowing gestures to historical time and the processes of decay and renewal. In the story Beckett establishes a conceptual network enfolding landscape and evidence of human intervention, combining geological time and human time (Neolithic, historic, and present time). This approximates what Tim Ingold has called a 'dwelling perspective', in which 'the landscape is constituted as an enduring record of – and testimony to – the lives and works of past generations who have dwelt within it' (Ingold, 1993, 152). Although Beckett's landscapes tend to lose their realist moorings in later prose narratives, his own record of writing comprises the records of 'past generations' of narrators and characters.

In counterpoint to agriculture, the landscape observed by Molloy in which A and C meet is sundered by natural forces. It is comprised of 'treacherous hills' with 'winding stones' seen 'from the summit of a monument' (*MY* 5). The familiar landscape recalls the view from Greystones across the Wicklow Mountains to the Irish Sea:

> From there he must have seen it all, the plain, the sea, and then these selfsame hills that some call mountains, indigo in places in the evening light, their serried ranges crowding to the skyline, cloven with hidden valleys that the eye divines from sudden shifts of colour and then from other signs for which there are no words, nor even thoughts. But all are not divined, even from that height, and often where only one escarpment is discerned, and one crest, in reality there are two, two escarpments, two crests, riven by a valley. (5–6)

The vocabulary characterizing this landscape implies violent forces transforming the earth, as though agriculture on a colossal scale. The mountains are serried – a military term from the Middle French *serre* ('close, compact') and ultimately from the Latin *serrare* ('to bolt, to lock') – that is, set one against the other; and they are 'cloven with hidden valleys' – where *cleave* stems from the Old English *cleofan* ('to split, to separate' but also 'to adhere to') and anticipates Clov in *Endgame*, his name resonating with the French *clou* or 'nail'; and the valleys *rive* the mountains, from the Old Norse *rifa* ('to tear apart') and ultimately from the Proto-Indo-European root *rei* ('to tear or cut'), anticipating the *rift* that will come to play such a critical etymological role in *Worstward Ho*. The topography of the landscape and the rich vein of etymology tapped by Beckett's narrator combine to illustrate how geography entails a complex network of temporal modes, enfolding the deep past as well as the historical past and the present. The elasticity of time finds its counterpart in space too, where geological and even global dimensions are invoked, at times improbably for comic effect, such as when the Unnamable rolls his way around the globe and back to his starting point.

Beckett's deep familiarity with the topography and history of the Wicklow Mountains is illustrated in a letter to Thomas McGreevy of 1 January 1935. Beckett describes his 'best days' walking the family dogs through the Wicklow Mountains, 'over the fields from here across the 3 Rock & 2 Rock & back by Glencullen & the Lead Mines' at Carrickgollogan, recalling memories of his father 'standing at the back of the Scalp' (*LI* 239), a rocky gap two miles north of Enniskerry. Topographically, human intervention in the form of open cut mining echoes the geological violence of the last glaciation which produced the region's deep valleys. The mines at Avoca date at least to the Bronze Age, and are where iron ore was extracted from as early as the twelfth century. From the eighteenth century, lead and copper became the principal minerals extracted from the region, although a significant gold rush occurred in the late eighteenth century (producing the largest gold nugget ever discovered in Britain and Ireland). The quarries at Ballyknockan produced granite used to build the Bank of Ireland Building on College Green in Dublin, the Dun Loghaire lighthouse that was to play a starring role in Krapp's epiphany, and other buildings such as Liverpool Cathedral. The quarries at Glencullen provided stone for the General Post Office building in O'Connell Street, a central site of the Easter Rising of 1916, and quarries at Dalkey and Barnacullia were also important for building works in Dublin. This history seeps into several of Beckett's narratives. In the opening scene of *Watt* Mr Hackett relates his early childhood in Glencullen, with his father 'out breaking stones on Prince William's Seat' invoking memories of 'the foothills to the dark bluff [where] he heard the distant clink of the hammers' (*W* 10, 11). Malone too recalls the quarries with 'the hearing of [his] boyhood' – he hears the dogs barking 'up in the hills, where the stone-cutters lived, like generations of stone-cutters before them' (*MD* 32). This memory takes on an almost sacramental tone: 'The stoniness of the sacred adds an unexpected dignity to Malone's death, a *gravitas* against which he struggles' (Keatinge, 2007, 328). Fittingly, the site of Golgotha itself was originally a quarry, in use between the seventh and first centuries BCE, thus giving the clinking of the hammers a Levantine and Christological shade (Finegan, 1992, 264).

Human statuary in Beckett's work provides a bridge between his varied use of stone, the tropes of archaeology, and his 'auto-speliology' or self-excavation. The figure of Memnon – invoking the two colossi flanking the tomb of Egyptian pharaoh Amenhotep III at Thebes – plays a critical role in this complex relation in *Ill Seen Ill Said*, having appeared serially throughout Beckett's oeuvre. Malone considers his avatar 'Jackson' as 'a stratum, strata, without debris or vestiges' (*MD* 53) and describes his posture as 'like that of the Colossus of Memnon, dearly loved son of Dawn' (54). *Fizzle* 7, 'For to end yet again', has a small figure 'erect still amidst his ruins all silent and marble still' (*TFN* 152), taking on the Memnon pose 'unbending as a statue' (153). The short prose text 'La Falaise' / 'The Cliff' has the human figure partially emerge from the rockface, only for 'Du coronal il tente encore de rentrer dans la roche' – the skull 'attempting to sink back its coronal into the rock' (*TFN* 163). Several of Beckett's stage characters share the physical attributes of statuary: the 'sad tale' told by the visitant to the nameless man in *Ohio Impromptu* (and narrated by the Reader to the Listener) is told 'a last time' with both figures sitting 'as though turned to stone' (*K* 140); and the Protagonist of *Catastrophe*, though pliable, is motionless but for his final act of defiance (*K* 147). These instances serve to blur notions of identity and motility, between human and stone, and between individual integrity and the physical stuff of artistic creation. Stone statuary also serves as a bridge to memory: in a letter to Thomas McGreevy of 4 August 1932 Beckett describes his childhood nurse 'Bibby' as having a visage 'the quality of ruined granite' (*LI* 113).

Ruins True Refuge

Beckett draws archaeological associations with literature as early as his short monograph on Proust. In a passage concerning Proust's view of friendship as a negation of the artistic spirit, Beckett frames the writing process as one where '[t]he only fertile research is excavatory, immersive, a contraction of the spirit, a descent' (*P* 65). In a later passage concerning artistic 'instinct' the artist supplies 'hieroglyphics traced by inspired perception', resulting in a 'work of art neither created nor chosen, but discovered, uncovered, excavated, pre-existing within the artist, a law of his nature' (*P* 84). Archaeological motifs imbue many of Beckett's works, providing him with an enduring network of associations by which to explore the constitution of characters and narrators, their understanding of memory, the use of intertextual reference (including between Beckett's texts), and the role of languages and the implications of etymology. These features align with some of the basic elements of archaeology: 'What the *excavating* archaeologist encounters is always a set of hybridized conditions such as mixed layers, superimposed structures, artifacts, stones, soil, and bones mixed together – in short, sites that object to modernity and historicism's wished-for ideal of completeness, order, and purified time' (Olsen, 2010, 127). Archaeology thus offers Beckett a critically self-aware discourse, where processes of writing become fictionalized – what Porter Abbott has called Beckett's *autography* or 'self-writing' (Abbott, 1996) – and where memory and historical residue in fictional form reflect back on how these functions operate textually, as objects and as durable events.

Beckett's characters' and narrators' propensity for graveyards, ruins, decayed objects, and stones advertizes the accretions of time that weigh upon them. When viewed from the position of archaeology, the present carries the cumulative residue of the past: 'Each of the moments of the past is indeed necessarily multi-temporal, since the present spontaneously becomes fossilized in being transformed; at any time, the present is made up of an accumulation of all the previous states whose successions have built this present "as it is now"' (Olivier, 2001, 66). The assemblage of objects in Beckett's texts, taken individually or collectively, press upon notions of human agency with their own forceful capacities, as well as their ability to reconstitute earlier material in Beckett's oeuvre. Archaeological objects thus function as actors in their own right, as outlined in Actor Network Theory (ANT): 'Instead of any central hero subjects – human, worldview, mind – we should envisage a brigade of actors: plates, forks, gravestones, humans, garbage pits, houses, food, chamber pots, law books, musical instruments, and so on acting together. [. . .] Thus, and not without a certain irony, the individual was made possible by the collective work of a brigade of actors' (Olsen, 2010, 145). Bjørrnar Olsen chooses an apt example to illustrate this point of the durable integrity of objects:

> A Neolithic pot used for storing food, left behind in an abandoned settlement from where it is recovered six thousand years later, retains some of its uniqueness and autonomy. Even when put on display in a faraway museum it is still a pot, not only holding in reserve its affordances and 'pot properties' for eventual (if unlikely) future actualization, but also persistently offering them for direct perception. (156)

Watt agonizes over the dislocation of word from thing in his meditation on the pot (*W* 67–9), but this scene may instead resituate the object at hand to function as a marker of historical continuity within the domestic economy of the Knott household. Despite Mr Knott's protean visage newly configured at each sighting, Watt reflects, in the Addenda, that 'Mr Knott too was serial, in a vermicular series' (*W* 222), deploying the earthy metaphor of the worm to signify historical and material continuity. Watt's pot is peculiarly apt, not only as a *locus classicus* for the excavating archaeologist, but also as a recurring trope of funereal fixity in such works as *The Unnamable, Endgame, Play, All Strange Away*, and *Imagination Dead Imagine*. The pot also opens into Beckett's intertextual play, recalling Thomas Browne's *Hydriotaphia, Urn Burial, or a Brief Discourse of the Sepulchral Urns Lately Found in Norfolk* (1658).

Archaeological tropes run through Beckett's work, stemming from his boyhood in the Wicklow Mountains among the Neolithic and Bronze Age stone formations. Beckett draws a link between archaeology and landscape as early as *More Pricks Than Kicks*, where the proliferation of archaic structures in 'Fingal' draws attention to the work of the Ordnance Survey of a century before, which found 'the Dublin mountains in ruins, its Gaelic heritage almost vanished' (Parsons, 2013, 93). Beckett makes this explicit by having the narrator draw out the etymology of Feltrim, 'The Hill of the Wolves' (*MP* 17): 'The appearance of the etymology announces the fact that this story will be uniquely concerned with antiquarian and archaeological pursuits, and will present the landscape as a palimpsest – under the fabric of the modern Dublin lie the traces of history' (Parsons, 2013, 94). The narrator of 'Fingal' elaborates: 'Abstract the asylum and there was little left of Portrane but ruins' (*MP* 23). In his diatribe to Watt, Arsene speaks of his desire 'to be turned into a stone pillar or a cromlech in the middle of a field or on the mountain side for succeeding generations to admire' (*W* 40), and in *The Calmative*, the posthumous narrator describes his den as 'just ruins, a ruined folly, on the skirts of the town, in a field' where 'the cows lie down at night in the lee of the ramparts' (*TE* 19). The ruins, '[c]yclopean and crenellated' (20), embody the archaeological affordance of 'being there' which allows for the 'gathering or sedimentation of the past' (Olsen, 2010, 160). The physical past of the land precedes the urbanized infrastructure in view across the field and ditch separating the ramparts from the city and provides the posthumous narrator a location from which to speak his own history. Ruins also populate such later prose works as *Lessness* – the first phrase, 'Ruins true refuge', sets the spare scene, followed by the second paragraph's opening phrase, 'Scattered ruins' (*TFN* 129) – as well as the eighth *Fizzle* 'For to end yet again', where sand 'pale as dust [. . .] engulf[s] the haughtiest monuments' (*TFN* 151) in a scene recalling Shelley's 'Ozymandias'. In *That Time*, Voice A recalls the 'ruin still there where you hid as a child' (*K* 99) and 'Foley's Folly bit of a tower still standing all the rest rubble' (100), and Voice C remembers sitting 'on the stone together in the sun on the stone at the edge of the little wood' (99). These enduring images of ruin illustrate time's work. In contrast, Beckett's essay for radio broadcast, 'The Capital of the Ruins', commemorates the town of Saint-Lô following Allied bombardment in the Battle of Normandy in June and July of 1944, written during Beckett's work for the Irish Red Cross as 'Quartermaster / Interpreter' in 1945–6 (Beckett, 1995, 275–8; see Knowlson, 1996, 345–8).

Beckett initially disparages antiquarian notions of Ireland's prehistory, but in later texts deploys its terminology in ironic counterpoint to any nationalist agenda. For Hamilton, Beckett's instigation of the language of antiquarianism tends to abstract any sense of a material excavation site, and thus any sense of continuity between ancient and modern epochs. Rather, 'Beckett's later prose, to varying degrees, regularly integrates fragments of antiquarian and archaeological terminology as the means to evacuate and confront realist modes of nationalist representation regardless of validity or accuracy'. By subverting the 'cultural sacredness' of the language of antiquarianism, Beckett 'allows the human remains to reverberate within a sepulchral-like space, producing a prose aesthetic instilled with a minimal amount of cultural reclamation as possible' (169, 171). The durability of Beckett's interests in these tropes, however, suggest that certain kinds of continuity are in play, whether the exhumation of the self beneath strata of experience and memory, or the agonistic relation of self to land via the index of human habitation across millennia.

Ontospeliology: the Geology of Consciousness

Beckett adapts the language of geology and archaeology into metaphors of the self in his fiction and drama. From as early as the 'Whoroscope' Notebook Beckett refers to the 'geology of conscience – Cambrian experience, cainozoic judgments, etc'. and composes an accompanying 'Table of Geological Eras' (62v) (Pilling, 2005, 46). The Cambrian period (581–485 million years ago) was the first geological period of the Paleozoic Era. The so-called 'Cambrian Explosion' saw the emergence of multi-cellular organisms and their development into early examples of all modern animal phyla. The Cainozoic or Cenozoic Era is the present era – the 'age of mammals' – dating from 66 million years ago, during which the continents moved into their present formations. Beckett's note forces a rough analogy between the Cambrian Period and early psychic life, and between the Cenozoic Era and a condition of consciousness turned, in part, to an attempt to understand those initial psychological foundations. This schema is turned to parodic use in the second *Watt* manuscript notebook: Arsene's diatribe – a far more extensive and baroque number than that preserved in Part 1 of the published text – veers into a cosmic waltz into the unconscious. The narrator explains his desire to leave Arsene in terms that conflate geological imagery with primal sexual ideation, 'trapped between [. . .] conical mammoth old red sandstone phalli and carboniferous pudenda':

> 'More!' said Arsene. 'Again! Again! Further! Deeper! The upper Silurian! The Lower Silurian! The truth! The truth!'
>
> [. . .]
>
> 'Plunge! Delve! Burrow! Deeper! Deeper! The Cambrian! ~~The pre-Cambrian! The truth!~~ The uterine! The pre-uterine'
>
> 'The pre-uterine' we said. 'No. That reminds us of the rocks at Greystones'. (Notebook 2 [MS-HRC-SB-6-5], leaf 79r)

Arsene plumbs the geological depths of the Paleozoic Era, moving from the Silurian period (444–419 million years ago) to the Cambrian, skipping over the intervening Ordovician period (485–444 million years ago). The Silurian period saw significant evolution in sea-life as well as multi-cellular life taking form on land (vascular plants and arthropods) following a series of Ordovician extinction events that wiped out sixty percent of all marine life forms. Arsene need not be apprised of these geological data to make his point that the Cambrian signifies the outer reaches of complex life and thus functions as an apt metaphor for 'the uterine'. The pre-uterine tips the scale into pure ideation in terms of human life – for Beckett the metaphorical twinkle in his father's eye, the father whose walking habits included Greystones, the location of his eventual burial.

The emergence of life – Beckett's own, by proxy of his narrator, as well as life across the geological record – is likened to lithic stratification and its geological analysis. Such matters of stratification translate to the documentary record of textual production: sequences of manuscripts, processes of revision, deletion, and emendation within specific documents, as well as transmission in publication stemmae. The affinities between evolution and textual production are evident in a shared vocabulary – genetic editions, stemmae, and so on – but the application of geology to the ways in which literary ideas and images develop and are evaluated retrospectively is especially pertinent: 'geology acts as a metaphor for the creative process, a means of accessing those "Profounds of mind" which yield inspiration' (Keatinge, 2007, 325). The mysteries of geological stratification haunt several of Beckett's narrators. Malone refers to his created alter ego as one of many strata (*MD* 53), and the Unnamable asks at the outset of his discourse: 'Are there other pits, deeper down? To which one accedes by mine? Stupid obsession with depth' (*U* 3). In an early draft of *Comment C'est* 'Beckett records and crosses out the word "Ontospéléologie," this time spelunking his way not just through the self but into the very caverns of being' (Wimbush, 2016, 5). Archaeological excavation, mining, and psychological depth are conflated in *... but the clouds ...* where V reports to have 'busied myself with nothing, that MINE' (*ATF* 140): 'The pun on mine [...] suggesting a connection between the "I" and a mine shaft through different layers not only shows congruence with the geology of consciousness, but also with one of Sigmund Freud's favourite metaphors: the "archaeology" of the mind' (Van Hulle and Nixon, 2013, 211–12).

Several of Beckett's characters and narrators pivot on the ambiguous distinction between internment (fixity, incarceration) and interment (burial). As Andy Wimbush has perceptively noted, Beckett's burlesque lecture in 1930 at Trinity College Dublin, 'Le Concentrisme', already demonstrates the implication 'that a mystic's meditative introspection, which plumbs the depths of mind and being, is analogous to a kind of geological excavation' (6). Belacqua expresses a wish to troglodize himself and be 'drawn down to the blessedly sunless depths' as a way of insulating himself from social expectations in *Dream of Fair to Middling Women* (*D* 122), having already figured his own mind as an inviting space for a bit of spelunking – 'all that inner space one never sees, the brain and heart and other caverns where thought and feeling dance their sabbath' (6). He elsewhere identifies consciousness in funereal terms – 'The mind suddenly entombed' (16) – similar to the Reader in *Ohio Impromptu* who tells of two seated figures '[b]uried in who knows what profounds of mind' (*K* 140). Malone speaks of 'the light that reigns in my den' (*MD* 46), and of his bed as a tumulus or 'barrow' (103). Krapp also locates himself in a den, where consciousness is a cavernous, even subterranean space. In *Texts for Nothing* 9, the narrator defies language to bury him in an avalanche of 'wordshit', then expresses the desire to find a way out that in turn leads down a 'long travelled road' to 'destination tomb' (*TFN* 37, 38). The conflation of tramping with death, the tomb with the mother – 'I'm dead and getting born' (38) – gives rise to a series of funereal images: 'hearse-horses' and 'the gates of the graveyard' (39). The following *Text* 10 brings this condition of neither life nor death to its apotheosis in the 'true sepulchral body' (*TFN* 42), an image that recurs slightly transformed as 'sepulchral skull' and 'cyclopean dome' in *Fizzle* 7, 'For to end yet again' (*TFN* 153), and recalls the 'ivory dungeon' of *Text* 2 (*TFN* 8). The 'dome' links architecturally with the 'beehive tombs' of *All Strange Away*: 'The term "Cyclopean" designates the Greek Mycenaean masonry style denoting monuments constructed of large boulders interlaced with smaller stones' (Hamilton, 2018, 170). The two ashbins in *Endgame* become funeral urns for Nagg and Nell, and Winnie in *Happy Days* is progressively interred in a barrow-like structure.

Burials and tombstones are often sites of inscription in Beckett's work, where narrators and characters believe that epigraphy may extend life beyond the biological body: 'The stone, always older than the words inscribed in it, is the principle of continuity of the words inscribed which are its occasion as an object of attention' (Dukes, 2016, 26). The notion of inscription as surrogate embodiment and posthumous legacy is a familiar literary trope, evident in Shakespeare's sonnets and elsewhere. But the merging of identity with lithic inscription belongs to the wider geological imagination at work in Beckett's texts. As he watches the two figures on the road below him, Molloy describes being seen by one of them in such terms: 'He gazed around as if to engrave the landmarks on his memory and must have seen the rock in the shadow of which I crouched like Belacqua, or Sordello, I forget' (*MY* 6–7). As the character James John Quin is fixed 'unmoved among the ruins' on leaf 19r in the first *Watt* notebook [MS-HRC-SB-6-4], he sees the 'lead letters' of his name 'stand on my tomb', and when he articulates his names they 'sounded softly within him, died and returned', bringing the organic and the lithic together in a moment of posthumous fantasy. Malone's story of the stone toward the end of his discourse suggests an indifference to death open to psychoanalytic reading: 'The neutral and inert properties of stone remind us of Freud's idea that, behind destructive human emotions, lies a desire to return to the inorganic' (Keatinge, 2007, 327).

In the posthumously published story 'Echo's Bones', the posthumous Belacqua 'sat on his own headstone, drumming his heels irritably against the R. I. P.' (*EB* 36) before meeting the groundsman Mick Doyle, who begins digging up the grave with his shovel and mattock. They lay a wager on the contents of the grave, and the coffin yields a 'handful of stones' (51), just as Echo's bones turn to stone in Ovid's rendering of the myth. The posthumous condition presented in the opening sentence of the story is one of excavatory peril, where the dead 'must take the place as they find it, the shafts and manholes back into the muck' (3).

Perhaps the starkest conflation of the human mind with burial chambers occurs in the later prose works *All Strange Away* and *Imagination Dead Imagine*. The former places in a progressively shrinking space first the protagonist, then a woman Emma, and finally an unnamed woman with memories of lying side by side with her companion. The dimensions are provided and emended, and a blazon is conducted upon Emma in a *deasil* or clockwise formation. The variation of light in the space, and its narrative malleability, induces the anology of the skull's interior, bolstered by the narrator's recourse to the word 'fancy' – a term favoured by William Wordsworth and William Blake, but defined as a secondary capacity of the human mind to that of imagination by S. T. Coleridge in chapter 13 of his *Biographia Litteraria*. By using the Scottish word *deasil* to indicate orientation, Beckett also draws attention to the archaic potential in his architecture. Passage graves such as New Grange used right-hand recesses as locations for valuable art, indicating 'a prehistoric appreciation of the priority of *dexter* over *sinister*, of *deiseal* over *tuathal*' (Herity, 1974, 123) – where *tuathal* is the Irish for counterclockwise, cognate with the Germanic *withershins*. Emma's 'ivory flesh' (*TFN* 77) resides within a 'rotunda three foot diameter eighteen inches high supporting a dome semi-circular in section as in the Pantheon in Rome or certain beehive tombs' (79). Beckett cites the prime examplar of rotunda architecture – Hadrian's second-century temple in Rome, still the world's largest unreinforced concrete dome – significant for its oculus, the round aperture in the middle of the ceiling that binds the temple's materiality to the heavens, and that allows light (and rain) into the building. *Rotunda* also describes a medieval Italian black-letter script (and later typeface) developed from Carolingian miniscule in order to facilitate the comprehension of the Vulgate Bible across Europe. The beehive tomb does not refer to the early medieval monastic *clocháns* of South-West Ireland but rather to the more ancient *tholoi* (θολωτόςτάφος or 'domed tombs') of Greece and Western Asia: *tholoi* on Crete date from the Early Minoan period (third millennium BCE), and elsewhere in Greece *tholoi* are generally Late Bronze Age constructions of the late second millennium BCE. These tombs are themselves often buried within a tumulus mound, with the *stomion* (doorway) and *dromos* (entrance) also covered with stones and earth, leaving the structure without any visible point of ingress or egress, with much of the chamber underground. *Imagination Dead Imagine* also introduces a rotunda: 'Diameter three feet, three feet from ground to summit of the vault [. . .] White too the vault and the round wall eighteen inches high from which it springs' (*TFN* 87). In this case the architectural analogy with the skull is made explicit, complete with a pun conflating shape and sound: 'a ring as in the imagination the ring of bone' (87). The constant light and heat in the space alternates between precise extremes, obviating any close analogy with ancient structures.

Beckett's geological imagination spans a wide range of figural and thematic instances across his writing career: stones and dispersed entities as mud, sand, and dust; topographical features given shape by the geological strata on which they rest; archaeological objects either decayed or buried; archaic structures such as *dolmens*, *cromlechs*, *clocháns*, and *tholoi*, or the ruined architecture of Wicklow found in towers, mottes, and crenellated walls; burial vaults and geological strata that signify the excavation of the self and the unconscious; and finally, the proxy archaeology of recycled textual fragments, citations from literary history, and the material status of manuscripts and letters both within his fiction and in the archive. These enduring features of Beckett's work are used strategically throughout his writing career, in narratives of generally increasing abstractness and reflexivity. The late prose of *Company, Ill Seen Ill Said*, and *Worstward Ho* signals a turn in Beckett's linguistic and tropological repertoire, where an intensification of geological imagery in the use of etymology and allusion comprises the same narrative ground as the explorations of subjectivity (and its limits) and the materiality of composition. These texts bring attention to the processes of their constitution as narratives, and in this sense they share a continuity with the narrative strategies of *The Unnamable* or *Texts for Nothing*. But in drilling into the very root and structure of language, these texts comprise a late-career meditation on the stratigraphic layerings of the English language over an extended writing career, and how these layers equally constitute an embodied record of writing in the textures of allusion to literary history and to Beckett's own oeuvre. By deploying figures of ruination and excavation, these late texts engage in radical modes of creativity evident in their narrators' capacities to create and destroy place and character. The rifts and ruins, the discovered strata, sherds, and ostraka in these texts also serve to recover textual memory, a process in contemporary archaeology that Bjørnar Olsen describes as 'a slow-motion archaeology, or self-excavation, that exposes the formerly hidden and black-boxed' (Olsen, 2010, 170). This memory work, embodied in the textual record of *Company*, *Ill Seen Ill Said*, and *Worstward Ho*, is Beckett's geological imagination.

2 *Company*: Mining Beckett's Literary Memory

The opening line of *Company* – 'A voice comes to one in the dark. Imagine' (*C* 3) – seems to dematerialize the geological and archaeological conditions undergirding Beckett's earlier writing. Vision contracts into darkness, and verbal communication displaces writing. The auditor and the reader are enjoined to engage with the voice via the faculty of imagination rather than the senses, whether we read 'Imagine' in the imperative mood ('Imagine!') or an implied conditional or interrogative mood ('Can you imagine?'). The second paragraph provides little more information concerning the location of the auditor 'on his back in the dark' (3) or of the issuing voice: no mud, ditch, mountain, or even an initial closed space, just a zone of occupancy 'in the dark'. Yet the word *imagine* bears a material history reaching past its Romantic associations as a creative metaphysical faculty. It returns to the grounding acts of artistic creation, the manipulation of stone, wood, and bone in the manufacture of figurative representation. Its etymology stems from the Proto-Indo-European root **aim* ('to copy, double'). The Latin *imaginari* ('to form an image') and *imago* ('image or likeness') entail a long history of Christian theology regarding the divine sculpting of humanity in God's image or likeness (*imago Dei*) (Boersma, 2016; Haslam, 2012). In psychology the *imago* also defines an idealized concept of a loved one formed in childhood, cognate with the Sanskrit यम (*yáma*, 'twin'). Thus to 'imagine' is to sculpt a twin in the memory, to craft a statue or talisman, but also to install one's own creative practice within the history of art, stretching back to the oldest known figurative artworks: the *Löwenmensch* (Lion-Man of Hehlenstein-Stadel) and the *Venus of Hohle Fels* dating to the early Upper Paleolithic Period (c. 35–40 000 BCE), discovered in German caves in 1939 and 2008 respectively. The fertile ground of *Company* comprises the archaeology of the mind, of memory, and of the creation of effigies in narration and intertextual reference as well as in memory and imagination. That Beckett should begin his story with an injunction to imagine – a key word in his late-career exploration of narrative objecthood – establishes his wider geological and archaeological repertoire in *Nohow On*: the statue or effigy is the focal object that unites ancient burial structures, gravestones, epigraphy, the excavatory work of literary allusion (especially of Romantic poetry), and the construction and erosion of narrative personae in both *Ill Seen Ill Said* and *Worstward Ho*.

The narrating voice quickly establishes the terms of this fictive world: true propositions are combined with unverifiable ones; the past tense dominates, but

gestures to the present and future also occur; the second-person pronoun signifies the voice and the third-person 'the cantankerous other' (4) to whom and
about whom the voice speaks. The grounds of imagination are reinforced by the
vocabulary of wonder: despite 'now even less than ever given to wonder' the
figure indeed wonders whether he is not alone (4), opening up potential worlds
within the otherwise diminished space, but also raising the possibility of his
own fictiveness (Tubridy, 2018, 191). Similarly the reduction of 'mind' pro-
vokes the voice to consider the conditions in which utterances are framed and
thus to invoke a metanarrative function: 'For were he merely to hear the voice
and it to have no more effect on him than speech in Bantu or in Erse then might it
not as well cease?' (5). Beckett's choice of languages mimics this movement
between utterance and its contemplation. Erse refers to the Goidelic Celtic
languages (Irish, Manx, and Scottish Gaelic), and Bantu designates several
hundred sub-Saharan languages (including Swahili, Zulu, Shona, and Xhosa)
belonging to the Niger-Congo language phylum: both terms describe language
groups rather than individual languages.

The narrative voice attempts to understand a schema of voices and address-
ees, bounded by what may be verified by the listener 'on his back in the dark'
and conditioned by what is imagined or wondered at. Numerous scholars have
tracked the shifts between various levels of narration and narrative self-
consciousness, including the 'middle voice' that straddles passive and active
registers, and the implications for what may be verified or surmised by the
auditor and therefore by the reader (Brown, 2016; Abbott, 1996; Barry, 2008).
These kinds of metanarrative inflections feature throughout Beckett's postwar
fiction, but *Company* exceeds a particular threshold where the fact of utterance
becomes the rift by which the terrain of fiction is measured: the geological
imagination becomes coexistent with the physical conditions of writing (the
page) as well as its intellectual conditions (the work of producing imaginative
space and entities to occupy that space, and the production of readers to
interrogate its features). Julie Beth Napolin identifies the rift that subtends
narrative utterance – the space of reading that opens up between the narrative
voice and its auditor or reader: 'Audibility is not a purely material category that
can be pluralized and distributed in a series as would a series of things: it is
the ontological force by which consciousness can experience itself as such'
(2017, 114). Derval Tubridy elaborates how pronouns are displaced in
a narrative that seeks out the 'origin of writing [. . .] before the artifices of
character and story', where the 'I' is an aporetic point of origin, deployed to
'abolish the intrusion of the "he"' by fusing it with the 'you' to whom the 'I'
makes his address (Tubridy, 2018, 178, 198). The disembodied voice also
makes manifest one of Beckett's enduring references: the figure of Echo in

Ovid's *Metamorphoses*. As Echo was condemned to living in caves (a geological formation familiar to Molloy), so the voice in *Company* resides in a closed, if undefined space, and is tormented, like so many of Beckett's protagonists, by the words of others (Campbell, 2001, 457, 459). The persistence of the Echo figure throughout Beckett's oeuvre transforms it, by the time of *Company*, into a material embodiment of its tropological force: a textual reverberation that leaves a residue of posthumous stones. The Echo trope becomes, in Thomas Hunkeler's formulation, an emblem of the subject of writing (*le sujet de l'écriture*) for Beckett (Hunkeler, 1997). The narrator of *Company* – like so many of Beckett's narrators before him – calls into being the narrated subject and the space in which the subject dwells, but does so on the basis of narrative being suspended over the rift separating voice from subject, filled with the work of memory and remnant intertextual fragments.

Beckett develops this textual rift by drawing on a range of biographical details in the narrative of *Company*. The voice shifts from the dark space of audition by recalling a memory of the auditor as a 'small boy' in Foxrock who exits from 'Connolly's Stores holding your mother by the hand', and the 'cutting retort' she makes to an innocent question concerning the colour of the sky (5–6). The narration returns to questions of its own constitution and the seriality of potential auditors, like the 'vermicular series' of Mr Knott's ancestors in *Watt* (*W* 222), or the servants who enter and exit his employ: 'If the voice is not speaking to him it must be speaking to another' (6). The pseudo-omniscient narrator then returns to the scene of childhood – 'You first saw the light in the room you most likely were conceived in' (7) – the room in Cooldrinagh with the bay window where both Sam and Frank were born and which 'looked west to the mountains. Mainly west. For being bow it also looked a little south and a little north. Necessarily. A little south to more mountain and a little north to foothill and plain' (7). The ensuing narration captures the biographical *mythos* surrounding Beckett's birth, when his father, with 'his love of walking and wild scenery', absented himself from the scene of labour and birth and instead took to tramping in the Wicklow Mountains (Knowlson, 1996, 15). In *Company*, the father relishes his lunchtime sandwiches 'looking out to sea from the lee of a great rock on the first summit scaled' (7), the topography replicated from such other narratives as *Texts for Nothing*. Beckett wrote to Thomas McGreevy on 2 July 1933 of his sorrow walking these roads following his father's death: 'I can't write about him, I can only walk the fields and climb the ditches after him' (*L1* 165). William Beckett was buried 'in a little cemetery on the Greystones side of Bray Head, between the mountains and the sea' (164), a prime position in Beckett's topography.

The narrative shifts abruptly after this recollection: 'You are an old man plodding along a narrow country road. You have been out since break of day and now it is evening' (9). The scene is created *ex nihilo*, demonstrating the tremendous world-giving powers of narration, yet the text is riven with references to Beckett's oeuvre (see Brater, 1983, 157–71; and Pilling, 1982, 127–31). The tramping figure echoes his own father's peregrinations (and William Beckett's) at the time of his birth and mimics the tramping figures in the *Fizzles* and elsewhere. Silence is broken only by 'footfalls' (8), each sound adding to a reservoir cognate with the cumulative weight of Beckett's oeuvre: 'add it in your mind to the growing sum of those that went before'. Progress is measured 'with bowed head on the verge of a ditch', recalling Watt's misadventure at the hands of Lady McCann, and in terms recalling the circumnavigatory exploits of the Unnamable – 'How often round the earth already' – where 'your father's shade' abides 'at your elbow during these computations' (8). This memory of the father is also an opportunity to recall the classical shades, particularly that of Anchises when Aeneas visits the underworld in Book 6 of *The Aeneid*. In the following paragraph the narrator mentions Beckett's birthdate of Good Friday, thus bringing into play Christ's visit to the shades in Limbo following his crucifixion (including his meeting with Joseph, his legal father). The Harrowing of Hell (*Descensus Christi ad Inferos*) is cited in Matthew 12:40, Romans 10:7, Acts 2:24–31, and 1 Peter 4:6, and recorded in the Apostles' Creed (Trumbower, 2001, 91–108). This narrative draws on the Hebrew concept of *sheol* (שְׁאוֹל) – the 'place of darkness' where all dead reside as 'shades' or *rephaim* – and features in early patristic works by Tertullian, Origen, Ambrose, and John Chrystostom. It also appears in a range of Anglo-Saxon texts (the early ninth-century Book of Cerne manuscript and the Homilies of Aelfric, for example) as well as in Canto 4 of Dante's *Inferno* and comprises the Byzantine artistic genre of the *Anastasis* (ἀνάστασις) later emulated by various Followers of Hieronymus Bosch, most famously in *Christ in Limbo* (c. 1575) in the Indianapolis Museum of Art.

The narrative weaves between memories closely resembling events in Beckett's life, on the one hand, and commentary on the scene of articulation, its physical conditions, and speculation on its affective force, on the other. Such augmented autobiographical memories from childhood include the 'old beggar woman [. . .] fumbling at a big garden gate' (9) who is not only '[h]alf blind' but also '[s]tone deaf', the adjective reinforcing the calcified strata of memory and recalling W. B. Yeats's figuration of Cathleen ni Houlihan; William Beckett enjoining his son to jump from the 'high board' at the Forty Foot promontory at Sandycove (10–11), where the mineralogical again makes direct contact with the workings of memory (the Forty Foot also appears in the first chapter of

Joyce's *Ulysses* and Flann O'Brien's 1939 novel *At Swim-Two-Birds*); and an adolescent encounter with a girl in his father's summerhouse at Cooldrinagh, a 'haven' and 'rustic hexahedron' (28) of 'seven cubic yards approximately' (29), reprising the closed spaces of *All Strange Away* and *Imagination Dead Imagine*. These imagined or recollected spaces embellish a purely literary or imaginative space cognate with the 'closed space' narratives, where the auditor may or may not be accompanied by 'his creature' (16) – shades of *Frankenstein* – and is configured to be 'huddled with his legs drawn up within the semicircle of his arms and his head on his knees' (17). The 'clenching and unclenching' hand (17) mimics the physical motions of Krapp feeling the dog's 'small, old, black, hard, solid rubber ball' (*K* 8) on the death of his mother, or the 'systole diastole' of the woman's pronated hands in *Ill Seen Ill Said* (60). *Company* excavates Beckett's earlier works for episodes and images drawn from his youth in Foxrock. In so doing, the narrative fuses the manifold operations of memory – Beckett's memories of his childhood and the reader's memory of these episodes from earlier texts – with the memorializing operations of the literary text in its quotations and allusions. Here Freud's 'archaeology of the mind' is realized as an archaeology of the text and its archival capacities.

The vocabulary of *Company* reinforces these bonds in the repeated use of the word *till*: 'Till one day', 'Till in the end' (10), 'Till having encountered' (32), 'Till it slowly flows again' (35). In each sentence the first word commences the process of tillage. The 'little void' in which the auditor abides also demarcates riven ground, a spatial relation with the earth that becomes an integral part of *Worstward Ho*. This echoes Demogorgon's final speech in Shelley's *Prometheus Unbound*, which begins 'This is the Day which down the void Abysm / At the Earth-born's spell yawns for Heaven's Despotism' and goes on to describe how love springs 'from the slippery, steep, / And narrow verge of crag-like Agony' (Act 4, 554–5 and 559–60 in Shelley, 1977, 209). Demogorgon is the 'supreme tyrant' of the shades in Shelley's closet drama, in which Earth is personified as the mother of all suffering and Prometheus is described in Christological terms: 'a youth / With patient looks nailed to a crucifix' (Act 1, 584–5, in Shelley, 1977, 153). This affinity between Demogorgon and Prometheus resonates with Beckett's relationship with his father, mediated by landscape. The 'crucified' Prometheus brings about the regeneration of humanity following the direction of the 'shade' Demogorgon, just as Beckett's narrator brings his subjects into being and the auditor is accompanied by his father's shade. Shelley's play, replete with mountains, crags, Prometheus's cave, and other geological formations, reflects upon the nature and weight of creativity.

As the narrator considers the ethics and modalities involved in creating 'the hearer M' and 'some other character' W, a similar return to earthy metaphors is invoked, with a nod to *How It Is*: 'Can the crawling creator crawling in the same create dark as his creature create while crawling?' (34). This incitement to quasi-philosophical or theological discourse is consistent with the text's recurrent invocation of Christ's crucifixion and the modality of the paternal 'shade'. The 'create dark' returns the reader to *Paradise Lost* cited early in the narrative, the 'darkness visible' in which '[s]ome soft thing softly stirring soon to stir no more' (11). The phrase refers to the vision of Satan's abode, the 'Dungeon horrible' in Book 1 of Milton's epic poem, while the sibilant iambic sentence that both precedes and follows recalls T. S. Eliot's phrasing of a similar precarious fragility in 'Preludes': 'I am moved by fancies that are curled / Around these images, and cling: / The notion of some infinitely gentle / Infinitely suffering thing' (2015, 16).

These images of fixity in the Underworld eventually give way to compulsive motion on the terrestrial plane. A narrated memory of compulsive tramping 'across the white pasture afrolic with lambs in spring and strewn with red placentae' (23) – a textual revenant that almost exactly replicates Arsene's utterance in *Watt* (*W* 38) and anticipates the woman's transit in *Ill Seen Ill Said* (64) – results in the thought of calculating the total number of 'footfalls' (23), as occurs in *Enough*. This intimacy with topography is captured in the description of each step as a moment of immobility – 'The foot falls unbidden in midstep or next for lift cleaves to the ground bringing the body to a stand' (24) – where *cleave* pivots on its meaning as an act of uniting (the foot with the ground) but also of division, indicating again how narrative topography discloses the deep rifts within memory as well as within and between texts. As the auditor crawls on hands and knees in the dark, counting each motion '[g]rain by grain ... [i]n what he hopes is a beeline' (32), this gesture of quantification recalls Hamm's 'impossible heap' of grains comprising his life (*E* 6). The figure seeks refuge from the dark by walking within 'a radius of one from home', accumulating 'some twenty-five thousand leagues or roughly thrice the girdle' (40), emulating the circumnavigatory feats of the Unnamable. The 'evermounting sum' (40) again recalls the perambulatory odyssey of *Enough*. This local wandering brings the purgatorial figure of Dante's (and Beckett's) Belacqua to mind, recumbent at the base of Mount Purgatory: 'sat waiting to be purged the old lutist cause of Dante's first quarter-smile' (40).

This network of memory, vocabulary, and intertextuality locates the style and imagery of *Company* in terrestrial and mineralogical strata. As Beckett's father (his 'deviser'), buried on the Greystones hillside, is transformed into a shade, so too the creative act of bringing these images into narrative actuality recognizes itself as a 'figment' of another's devising: 'Devised deviser devising it all for company' (30). The modern usage of 'devise' – to form, invent, or fashion – dates to the Middle English *devisen*, which itself stems from the Latin *diviso*. An archaic English usage bears the meaning 'to imagine', the very act or instruction provided at the outset of *Company*. Another Middle English usage has the noun *devise* mean 'the act of bequeathing by will', circling back to the father/shade and son/tramper, and to Beckett's anguish at walking the hillsides his father bequeathed to him, as well as to his memorializing their shared inheritance in *Company*. Each deviser is equally devised, is equally creator and creature, and in the act of devising – creating figments out of the terrain, from the Latin *figmentum*, 'fiction' – functions as a devise of inheritance. The theological echoes resounding in such terms of creation culminate in one of the final intertextual references in *Company*: an instruction to the auditor to remain supine, never again to rise and 'bow down your head' at the point when 'words are coming to an end' (46). A crucial instance in chapter 12 of Ecclesiastes – which opens with the command to '[r]emember now your creator' (12:1) – captures this apocalyptic tone by referring to difficult times ahead, 'when the keepers of the house tremble, / And the strong men bow down' (12:3). Beckett also draws on Psalm 145:14 in *All That Fall*, when Mrs Rooney announces the preacher's text for the religious service the following day: 'The Lord upholdeth all that fall and raiseth up all those that be bowed down' (*ATF* 30). Creation and decreation weave together in the acts of the artificer.

Company is equally sensitive to the linguistic heritage of modern English. The question 'Whence the shadowy light?' recalls the mysteries of illumination in *The Lost Ones* and the unpublished story fragments 'Long Observation of the Ray' – the saltatory light fossilized in *Company* in the 'abrupt saltation' (20) of the voice's movements in the dark. The question also anticipates *Worstward Ho* in the use of Anglo-Saxon words to orient in space and time ('whence', 'wither', 'thence', and 'thither') and recalls other non-Latinate terms of direction such as the Middle Low German *withershins* (28, 36) for anticlockwise, and the Scottish Gaelic *deasil* for clockwise from *All Strange Away* and *Imagination Dead Imagine*. The text complicates this linguistic heritage by its controlled mixing of Latinate, Germanic, and Greek words:

> Another trait the flat tone. No life. Same flat tone at all times. For its affirmations. For its negations. For its interrogations. For its exclamations. For its imperations. Same flat tone. You were once. You were never. Were you ever? Oh never to have been. Be again. Same flat tone. (13)

The 'same flat tone' presents a riddle to the narrator: both 'same' (*sami*) and 'flat' (*flatr*) entered Middle English from Old Norse, but 'tone' made its way into Middle English from Greek τόνος and Latin *tonus*, and ultimately from the Proto-Indo-European **ten*, meaning 'to stretch'. The contrast between the lifeless tone and the rhetorically florid content elicits a series of anaphoric statements with exclusively Latinate words. This repeats a prominent pattern in *The Lost Ones*: whenever the narrator lacks understanding of the conditions of the cylinder, he seeks recourse in Latinate vocabulary – 'commutator', 'certitudes', 'maximum', 'minimum', 'vibration', 'stridulence', '*mutatis mutandis*' – in an attempt to shore up narrative control. This aspiration fails, where the narrator of *Company* gives way to affective speech using a Germanic vocabulary – 'Oh never to have been' – and reprises the opening phrase in a gesture of inevitability: 'Same flat tone'.

Anglo-Saxon words predominate in matters of topography and earth, and Latinate words tend to accumulate in passages of measurement or the pursuit of empirical certainties. *Company* contains more exclamations than any other of Beckett's texts except perhaps *Worstward Ho* – 'Over!' (8), 'One day!' (10), 'What visions in the dark of light!' (39), 'Home!' (40), 'What an addition to company that would be!' (12, 17, 18, 40) among others. Similarly, the interjection 'Aha!' (33) draws attention to the affective state of narration, citing the strategic placement of similar expressions in the establishing sentence of *Imagination Dead Imagine* – 'pah' (*TFN* 87) – and Arsene's various ejaculations – 'Haw!' – in Part 1 of *Watt*. The narrator deploys 'quick' throughout *Company* in relation to how the narrative subject is to be treated – 'Quick leave him' (3, 15, 30, 40) – or as a prompt to narration – 'Quick imagine' (21). This word also plays a role in establishing narrative authority in *Ill Seen Ill Said* – 'Quick enlarge and devour' (55), 'Quick again to the brim the old nausea' (64), 'Quick the eyes' (65), 'Quick blacken' (75), 'Quick beforehand again two mysteries' (76) – combined with other repeated imperatives – 'Careful' (45, 59, 65, 70, 73), 'On' three times alone in the first paragraph (45), and 'Gently gently' (48, 60, 71). Quick also plays a pivotal role in Beckett's geological imagination: descending from the Proto-Indo-European root **gwei* ('to live') and entering Old English as *cwic* ('alive', from which derives the phrase 'the quick and the dead'), a Middle English usage for *quick* pertained to the instability of gravel pits and shifting soil. Quick: to be alive but precariously so; living on the shifting ground of fortune or an unseen narrator's whim.

Company performs an enigma of speaking and listening, being and acting, where as many as five subjects may be present in the narrative act – the voice, its listener (W), 'that cantankerous other' (M), 'another still [. . .] Unnamable' (15), as well as the implied reader – but equally where a single entity may have fabricated the entire story into this unlikely expression of sociability, a gallery of effigies. *The Unnamable* presents a similar problem in which the reader must deliberate on whether '[a]ll these Murphys, Molloys and Malones' are figments of the Unnamable's narration or whether they in turn are real and control him (*U* 14). This choice between persecution by the mob and the creation of unruly figments can be resolved by recasting character and narrative as the material by which the narrator's mind finds expression in its creation of narrative space and textual ground. *Company* casts its vocabulary across Beckett's prose and drama, and across a range of literary texts, where references semi-submerged and fossilized await the archaeologist-reader. These deployments of intertextuality and autobiographical reference perform a fictionalized 'ontospeliology' or excavation of being. These textual shards and fragments constitute a world for the auditor – a world based on sound rather than sight, and affective memory rather than a procession of historical milestones and material evidence. The notion of the memory as a buried coffer storing textual fragments is made material in *Ill Seen Ill Said*, where voice, vision, and dwelling each provide the grounds for an excavatory poetics.

3 *Ill Seen Ill Said*: Turning Deasil among the Cromlechs

Mal vu mal dit / *Ill Seen Ill Said* shifts from the mining of consciousness and memory in *Company* to the translations between human subjectivity and lithic objecthood, between the powers of narration to bring a world into being and the objects of that world to assert themselves as independent actants. The scenario is of an external observer's view of a lone woman in a remote hovel surrounded by standing stones and pastures beyond. The narrating voice seems to devise this habitus – 'The cabin. Its situation. Careful. On. At the inexistent centre of the formless place' (*I* 45–6) – such that the narrator deliberates over whether the woman is to be alive or dead: 'No shock were she already dead. As of course she is. But in the meantime more convenient not' (73). This narratological power recalls several of the 'closed space' narratives such as *Imagination Dead Imagine*, *Ping*, and *The Lost Ones*. Yet the peering eye (the 'eye of prey') is not privy to the woman's affective states and can only infer her state of mind through her actions. This mutual implication of mind, perception, narration, and world grounds the narrative in quite literal ways: the standing stones or 'twelve' surrounding the 'hovel' provide mobile anchor points by which to ground the woman's movements as they follow her across her terrain. Other mineralogical forces become evident in the white stones spread across the terrain, the headstone of the grave the woman ritually visits, and the presence of Venus, a terrestrial planet, in the evening sky. The hovel itself is considered in quasi-archaeological terms, and the ground upon which the narrative is based comes into focus as the grounding of language. This is accomplished through the narrator's intensive mode of intertextual reference, including reference to Beckett's works, and by the increasing use of archaisms as the narrative proceeds. *Ill Seen Ill Said* was the only text of *Nohow On* to have been composed first in French and then translated into English. Charles Krance notes that the translation into English began very early in the composition process – although the larger part was undertaken after *Mal vu mal dit* had been submitted to the printer (Krance, 1996, 162–5 and 195–8) – where Beckett's philological predilections are given more intensive focus in English than in French. Its effectiveness in shifting from the scene of consciousness in *Company* is due to the role of geology and archaeology, where excavations of earth and stone match those of literary precedent and language.

Mooring Celestial Objects

The opening sentence balances the weight and fixity of terrestrial moorings with celestial objects: 'From where she lies she sees Venus rise. On'. (45). The woman observes 'the star's revenge' on darkness in the guise of Lucifer, 'the radiant one' (45) or 'light bringer', thereby invoking a rich intertextual resonance: Beckett invokes the Latin Vulgate Bible's translation of the Hebrew הֵילֵל (*helel*). The King James Bible identified this name for Venus with that of Satan, the principal fallen angel, an identification later assumed by John Milton in *Paradise Lost*. Such Bronze Age personifications of Venus as the Sumerian Inanna, the Babylonian Ishtar, and the Phoenician Astarte, each of whom strive for the highest place in heaven only to be cast into the underworld, reflect the discontinuous presence of Venus in the visible sky (Cooley, 2008, 164–5). Beckett's use of internal rhyme is magnified in the triple rhyme in the next long sentence: 'From where she lies when the skies are clear she sees Venus rise'. These poetic devices are punctuated by the imperative command 'On' – issued by Pozzo to Lucky in *Waiting for Godot* and the first word of *Worstward Ho*. The figure of Venus also draws on Beckett's lifelong interest in astronomy, evident in the *Dream* Notebook (1999, 145–50, items 1040–67) in which he recorded a sequence of notes and quotations from Sir James Jeans's *The Universe Around Us*, mostly from its first chapter, 'Exploring the Sky' (Jeans, 1929, 1–88).

These brief glimpses of Venus ground Beckett's narrative within a geological discourse in relation to other celestial objects such as the moon, the light from which illuminates the stones of all shapes and sizes scattered across the 'zone of stones' (47). Venus is a celestial rock, one of four terrestrial planets in the solar system, and due to its size and density – if not its atmosphere and periods of rotation and revolution around the sun – is often referred to as earth's sister planet. The narrative returns to a vision of Venus only once more, when the woman's tears are shed observing 'the white heap of stone' aspiring to 'gain the skies. The moon. Venus' (57). This makeshift Tower of Babel seeks out the two dominant terrestrial objects in the sky before Venus is eventually banished '[f]or good' (60). The two spheres of sky and earth are clearly demarcated: the former has its darkness punctuated by stars; while the latter is distinguished by the white stones and white cabin walls set against darkness, where the elements of stone and frozen water invoke the workings of geological time. These images and references operate on glacial and astrogeological scales – marking out the woman as a product of the history of rock formation and erosion. Her 'becoming rock' provides a posthuman aspect to the narrative, where physical evidence of human emotion ('scalding' tears falling where previous tears are long frozen) gesture toward the dialectical relationship she seems to inhabit with the twelve standing stones.

Strange Attraction: Stone Woman

If the story's drama resides in the woman's movements between her abode and the landmarks surrounding it, and the invasive narrative surveillance to which she is subject, the presence and agency of the twelve standing stones function as powerful counterparts. Peter Boxall maps out the terrain between the woman's hut, the surrounding 'zone of stones', the pastures beyond, and the undefined 'paradise' or outer zone, noting the inherent fuzziness in these topological demarcations, where 'looking erodes the very boundaries between zones upon which vision depends' (Boxall, 2009, 161). This observation shifts the emphasis away from deciding whether such fuzziness is ontological or epistemological. Instead the burden rests upon visual perception, both within the narrative frame (the woman's perception as well as the narrator's) and in how the reader 'sees' the story's topography. Boxall discerns a concentric topography, with hovel, stones, pastures, and 'paradise' mimicking the topography of megalithic stone circles, not least in the way the hovel's architecture echoes the orientation of ancient tombs towards major celestial events in the arc between the limits of sunrise and moonrise in the northeast and southeast. The woman's odyssey consists partly in traversing the 'imaginary boundary lines' demarcating each zone, and in resisting the way the stones and the 'haze' threaten to overwhelm both her and the landscape in an all-consuming white or dark (Boxall, 2009, 157).

This appeal to the inorganic as an alternate form of animation not only returns the reader to Beckett's childhood and his recuperation of stones to the refuge of his tree at Cooldrinagh, but also to the ancient topography of the Wicklow

Mountains. The cromlech of Glen Druid is a Neolithic source of reference for Beckett (O'Brien, 1986, 27 and 29). It functions more as a model for a tomb or enclosed space, a 'true refuge', rather than as any direct reference to the standing stones in the narrative, and thus could be described as a distributed reference between the hovel and the gravesite visited throughout the narrative. Megalithic archaeology becomes an especially acute source of the story's imagery mediating the human and the inorganic: 'while Beckett resists the Romantic tendency to invest the landscape with personality or to see it as a reflection of the human soul, he does respond to its mineral and inorganic qualities, finding here, perhaps, the traits which render it separate from the human realm' (Keatinge, 2007, 323).

The deep association between the woman and stone is established early in the narrative. She is 'drawn' to a particular location where 'stands a stone' (48), a '[r]ounded rectangular block three times as high as wide. Four' (48), the headstone of her beloved's grave. The fundamental ambiguity in this human–lithic relation is conveyed grammatically: 'It it is draws her' is most cogently read as 'it is this stone, that draws her to this spot'. Yet the repetition of 'it' also allows for such variations as 'the essence, thisness or *haecceity* of the stone, its unique indivisibility, affords it the power to draw the woman' where 'to draw' is to attract but also to create, as a narrator 'draws' a character. As the stone compels her journey across the terrain – 'she must to it', 'she could find her way' blindfolded – she reflects its immobility as she halts before it, 'as if of stone'. This relation between the human agent and the grave marker unites the physical process of burial and the psychological process of mourning: 'The analogy between these two parallel rites of internment rests on an intimate and age-old kinship between the earth and human inwardness – a kinship that makes the earth the caretaker of cultural memory and cultural memory the caretaker of the earth' (Harrison, 2003, 50). The capacity of the grave marker to function as a signification of mortality also affords it the ability to create a sense of place:

> It is not for nothing that the Greek word for 'sign', *sema*, is also the word for 'grave'. For the Greeks the grave marker was not just one sign among others. It was a sign that signified the source of signification itself, since it 'stood for' what it 'stood in' – the ground of burial as such. In its pointing to itself, or to its own mark in the ground, the *sema* effectively opens up the place of the 'here', giving it that human foundation without which there would be no places in nature. (20)

Liddell and Scott give the definition of σῆμα as 'sign, mark, or token' a 'sign from heaven, omen', 'constellation', as well as a 'sign by which a grave is known, mound, cairn, barrow' (Liddell and Scott, 1950, 1592). The demarcation of place is brought into view mineralogically by the stone slab at the threshold of the woman's house, the standing stones in their mysterious motions, but above all the headstone which functions as a gnomon or point of orientation, grounding potential signification and therefore narrative meaning. She takes on the characteristics of the stone marker, and it becomes an animating object governing her action: 'when the stone draws then to her feet the prayer, Take her' (48). The woman's lithic visage also recalls the figure of Echo, whose bones, Ovid records in his *Metamorphoses*, turn to stone when she is spurned by Narcissus and dies from grief – a process cognate with that undertaken by the woman of *Ill Seen Ill Said*. This reference bore substantial significance to the younger Beckett, whose poem 'Echo's Bones' lends its title to his first collection of poems, and which is repeated in the title of the posthumously published prose coda intended for *More Pricks Than Kicks*.

The woman 'consents at last' to have her features examined by the narrating voice / eye, which blends the woman's face with the stones that hold her in their thrall: 'Calm slab worn and polished by agelong comings and goings. Livid Pallor. Not a wrinkle. How serene it seems this ancient mask' (56). This mask becomes the subject of a blazon: the 'washen blue' of the eyes, the 'lids occult', and the lashes 'jet black' are pronounced by virtue of the woman's tears; she is twice described as 'once a brunette'; and '[s]kipping the nose at the call of the lips these no sooner broached are withdrawn' (56). This poetic convention – enlivened with archaisms ('washen'), assonance ('Lashes jet black'), alliteration ('Time will tell', 'not for nothing'), and ambiguous agency in the absence of prepositions – merges with the subsequent description of the flagstone in the diminishing light: 'The slab having darkened with the darkening sky. Black night henceforward. And at dawn an empty place'. This threshold stone is placed at the epistemological limit, occupying the initial condition of the woman's absence, but without betraying whether she returned home or, 'under cover of darkness', continued her 'ways' (57).

This blurring of the human and the inorganic extends beyond the woman's immovable face to other moments, '[m]erely frozen' (62), of extreme immobility. She is given grandiose iconographic status in taking on 'again the rigid Memnon pose' (63) as she sits with her spoon and bowl. This reference to the two colossi guarding the mortuary temple of the Egyptian pharaoh Amenhotep III (ruled c. 1386–1349 BCE) at Thebes recalls its usage in *Malone Dies* and *The Unnamable*. This association with male statuary and nominally male characters in Beckett's earlier fiction not only blunts gender identification but converges the human and the mineralogical: a dynamic relation that Jonathan Boulter has recently described as making *Ill Seen Ill Said* a 'parable of posthuman space' (Boulter, 2019, 155–96). Conor Carville notes the historical associations of these figures, particularly in pictorial representations: 'Highly evocative images of these enormous sitting figures, their outlines and profiles porous and ruined by time, had been circulating in French print culture since Napoleon's Egyptian campaign in 1798' (Carville, 2018, 225). Beckett's fascination with Egyptian statuary on visits to Berlin also informs these associations – Beckett refers to 'ein bärtige Sphinx' ('a bearded sphinx') in the Tell Halaf Museum in Berlin in a letter to Günter Albrecht on 31 December 1936 (*L1* 409) – and invokes the remnant image of colossal statuary in Shelley's poem 'Ozymandias'. As the reader is enjoined to compare the woman's ghostly smile with 'true stone', and the narrative scene is progressively overtaken by 'Universal Stone' (72, 73), the Memnon pose serves as a kind of geological distinction. The Colossi of Memnon are made of quartzile sandstone, and while the Wicklow Mountains are composed largely of a granite batholith, this rests upon a substrate of quartzile sandstone formed during the Cambrian period of 542–488 million years ago, when the entire area was deep underwater in the primeval Iapetus Ocean. Wicklow's topography of solid igneous rock is undergirded by ancient sedimentary rock – a reminder of changeability beneath the apparent fixity of things. Geological change and the woman's figural metamorphosis throughout the narrative are cognate processes. The latter is modulated by the narrative eye and its fallibilities, as well as the literary associations its voice cannot help but introduce into the text.

The temptation to read the terrain of *Ill Seen Ill Said* as Wicklow is mitigated by an early clue steering the reader away from the 'neatness' of this association. The terrain is described as though a scene in a Caspar David Friedrich land-scape: 'Chalkstones of striking effect in the light of the moon' (46), where the illuminated 'zone of stones' shows '[i]nnumerable white scabs all shapes and sizes' due to the 'chalky soil' (47). The presence of chalkstone, or calcium carbonate, is more often associated with the Southern England Chalk Formation including such iconic landmarks as the Needles off the Isle of Wight, the white cliffs of Dover, and various chalk hill figures in Dorset and Wiltshire. Yet chalk fits here: calcite is formed from the submarine compaction of coccoliths or shells of microorganisms, thus making it a product of organic matter and geological forces. Chalk is where the organic and inorganic not only meet but are mutually constitutive. It is fitting that the soil and lawn of the 'zone of stones' should yield to these chalky tessellations.

Further riches are hidden within the emergent chalkstone. Isaiah 27:9 in the King James Bible has the prophet outline the cleansing of Jerusalem in prepar-ation for the Day of Judgement: 'By this therefore shall the iniquity of Jacob be purged; and this is all the fruit to take away his sin; when he maketh all the stones of the altar as chalkstones that are beaten in sunder, the groves and images shall not stand up'. In the text's historical context this purity refers to the Kingdom of Judah repelling the predations of the Assyrians. The Hebrew term אֶבֶן גִּר (*Eben gir* or *Yaban gir*) designates chalkstone or limestone, and *gir* also refers to the lime plaster on which the hand writes at Belshazzar's feast in Daniel 5:25 – מנא מנא תקל ופרסין (*mene mene tekel upharsin*) – the fateful moment of judgment to which Hamm alludes in *Endgame*. Chalkstone objects commonly unearthed in Jerusalem's archaeological sites include private domestic ritual baths, due to the stone's symbolic role as a purifying agent and its imperviousness to ritual defilement in ancient Jewish law (Gordon, 2019, 56). Cement comprised of crushed limestone heated with other minerals provided the Romans with strong building materials for such structures as the Pantheon and the Coliseum. Thus chalkstone, in its historical uses and etymological associations, unites empires (Roman, Assyrian, Babylonian) and the oppressed and captive Israelites in one binding image. Lime is also used for more mundane purposes such as the binding agent in wattle and daub structures and whitewash, linking the mineral deposits beneath the woman's feet with the walls of her dwelling.

An abiding mystery (or 'sphinx') of the topography in *Ill Seen Ill Said* is the motility of the standing stones, in contrast to the fixity of the headstone to which the woman makes habitual pilgrimage. Beyond the inner zone of stones, the twelve standing stones 'furnish the horizon's narrow round' (47). These stones, '[a]lways afar', appear to the woman's vision to be continually receding – 'She never once saw one come toward her. Or she forgets. She forgets' – to the point where she asks herself, or the narrator imagines she asks herself, 'Are they always the same? Do they see her?' (47). In a tableau of apparent calm the woman is seen from behind as she sits on the white stones, facing the standing stones on her horizon. This scene makes dense allusion to Beckett's prose oeuvre, and it unites the three kinds of stone in the narrative: the scattered 'zone of stones' in which the woman is located; the standing stones ever receding before her; and (as inferred by the narrator) the grave marker in her desire to 'go and stand still by the other stone' (59). This scene follows on from the woman having visited the 'tomb', where in her frozen visage of repressed emotion 'she seems turned to stone' (58), and a brief moment inside her hovel in which she '[s]tares as if shocked by some ancient horror', her face 'stone-cold' (58), invoking the classical topos of the Medusa stare, who turns her victims to stone.

The woman's observation of 'the twelve' combines biological and geological timescales. The stones 'keep her in the centre' (55) but are not her captors, as they form a ring 'whence she disappears unhindered' (55). Indeed it seems the woman is the ascendant force, shaping the flow of time in the rapidity or otherwise of her movements: 'time slows all this while. Suits its speed to hers' (56). This temporal relation with the standing stones – products of human labour – contrasts with the accelerated geological time prevailing in the 'field of stones', where processes of erosion and the emergence of 'plentiful' white stones from the earth take place (57).

> From the stones she steps down into the pastures. As from one tier of a circus to the next. A gap time will fill. For faster than the stones invade it the other ground upheaves its own. So far in silence. A silence time will break. This great silence evening and night. Then all along the verge the muffled thud of stone on stone. Of those spilling their excess on those emergent. Only now and then at first. Then at ever briefer intervals. Till one continuous din. (57-8)

Beckett again plays on the agricultural meaning of 'till', combining an earthen image with a measure of time. The stones illustrate geological processes in a human timescale, and the woman in turn mimics the lithic condition: 'Frozen true to her wont she seems turned to stone' (58).

The woman's visage and stature become stone-like but she resists becoming 'pure figment': 'Her stubborn persistence to be seemingly always there, even when the eye is not looking, preserves her as if frozen in time and the space circumscribed by the fragmentary protocols of *Ill Seen Ill Said*' (Langlois, 2017, 217). As an object that both anchors and stands outside the narrator's ken, the woman stands apart from any 'deviser', but she is a figment in the most fundamental sense. Derived from the Latin *figmentum* ('be formed, contrived') and ultimately from the Proto-Indo-European root **dheigh* ('to form, to build'), its root also produces the Old English *daege* ('female servant, housekeeper') as well as the Latin *effigies* ('copy, imitation, likeness, statue') from which the modern English *effigy* derives. Thus the woman – perhaps once a servant or housekeeper – is a figment in the sense that she is a quasi-archaeological representation, statue-like in her immobility and affinity with the standing stones, contrived by the narrator despite her grounded essence resisting complete domination. Her hands are even observed to possess a 'faintly leaden tinge' (60), with the missing third finger – the 'keeper' – on the left hand inducing a rhythmic lithic vision: 'Still as stones they defy as stones do the eye' (61). Her inertia matches the slowing of the terrain: 'The gradual becoming-stone of the landscape [...] is cast as a kind of calcification, a kind of freezing, in which the trembling is finally stilled' (Boxall, 2009, 158 and 159).

The narrator is unable to approach the woman as a human subject: she is an effigy, stone-like, a rock or statue. The ill-seeing 'treacherous eyes' see her 'vanishing' into the haze that 'reigns beyond the pastures' and that becomes the 'sole certitude' (70). The 'drivelling scribe' compares her to 'true stone', aware that the entire scene tends to the condition of 'Universal stone' (72). The collapse of the visual field is first broached in a scene of falling snow, where the Twelve are 'obliterated' but still present: 'Invisible were she to raise her eyes' (61). In a late scene she is accompanied by another figure, their shadows cast by the sun that 'stands still' only to 'recoil' when they part, 'its face over the pastures and then the stones the still living shadow slowly glides' (69). Yet the focal point of narratological uncertainty resides in the gravestone:

> Changed the stone that draws her when revisited alone. Or she who changes it when side by side. Now alone it leans. Backward or forward as the case may be. Is it to nature alone it owes its rough-hewn air? Or to some too human hand forced to desist? As Michelangelo's from the regicide's bust. If there may not be no more questions let there at least be no more answers. Granite of no common variety assuredly. Black as jade the jasper that flecks its whiteness. On its what is the wrong word its uptilted face obscure graffiti. Scrawled by the ages for the eye to solicit in vain. Winter evenings on her doorstep she imagines she can see it glitter afar. When from their source in the west-southwest the last rays rake its averse face. Such ill seen the stone alone where it stands at the far fringe of the pastures. (67–8)

The stone displays its weathered history on its face, a condition guided by a human hand just like Michelangelo's incomplete tomb of Pope Julius II – 'the regicide's bust' – intended for St. Peter's Basilica but instead located in San Pietro in Vincoli on the Esquiline Hill in Rome. The analogy is heavily ironic, with the stone's 'rough-hewn' human intervention contrasting with Michelangelo's colossal Papal commission in 1505, interrupted by Bramante's redesign of St. Peter's and by the commission of the Sistine Chapel ceiling (1508–12) but still a source of several iconic sculptures. Michelangelo's *Moses* (1513–15) was intended for the original tomb and now stands alone in San Pietro in Vincoli, as were the *Dying Slave* and *Rebellious Slave* (c. 1513–16), both in the Louvre in Paris, as well as the four unfinished *Slaves* now in the Galleria dell'Accademia in Florence. The humble gravestone is presumed to be granite – the underlying stone of the Wicklow Mountains – flecked with black jasper, a prized gemstone across the ancient civilizations of Persia, Greece, Rome, and Assyria. The narrator draws attention to the 'obscure graffiti' on the headstone, sending the reader back into Beckett's epigraphic archive in *Watt*, *Echo's Bones*, and elsewhere. Where the narrator's field of vision is obscured, the woman's sight is tinted by her imagination: the glittering stone binds the zone of stones, the pastures, and 'paradise' beyond this 'fringe', by means of its totemic role in her panoramic view.

Abode of Things

The topographic field of *Ill Seen Ill Said*, with its chalk scars, granite, slate, and other minerals, directly speak to Lucky's 'abode of stones' in *Waiting for Godot*. The woman's abode, perhaps a humble whitewashed wattle and daub dwelling, is an abode of things that repeatedly demonstrate their relation to the earth and the mineralogical realm. Not only is her 'cabin' hemmed in by stones and graced by a flagstone that bears proof of her constant movement in its worn surface, but its contents persistently assert their geological origins. The minimal furnishings of 'a pallet and a ghostly chair' (49), the curtains across the two windows, and the two skylights in the pitched roof defer to the small objects populating the space. The woman's preparations to leave have her 'ill-button' her boots with the aid of a 'buttonhook larger than life' (52). This object immediately takes on Christian associations in its form as well as the method of its suspension: 'Of tarnished silver pisciform it hangs by its hook from a nail. It trembles faintly without cease. As if here without cease the earth faintly quaked' (52). Ancient Ireland was a centre for gold mining but not silver, suggesting the pisciform buttonhook was produced in Britain, a site of silver production since Roman times. Whether the reader is meant to assume the trembling of the buttonhook as a measure of its precarious thinghood – its own 'trembling' likened to seismic activity of extremely rarity in Ireland – or else the product of ill-seeing, the silver itself is given the same attribute as the stones and the moonlight: 'Silver shimmers some evenings when the skies are clear' (52) and 'The buttonhook glimmers in the last rays' (54).

This scene opens up a number of avenues for thinking about the integrity of objects. The worn buttonhook – 'The shank a little bent leads up to the hook [. . .] A lifetime of hooking has lessened its curvature [. . .] Since when it hangs useless from the nail' (52) – invites comparison with Heidegger's evaluation of the peasant's shoes in Vincent Van Gogh's painting *A Pair of Shoes* (1885) in his essay 'The Origin of the Work of Art' (Heidegger, 1993, 143–212). In this way the buttonhook can be seen as a kind of *world* encompassing all the relations that have produced its present condition, and part of *earth*, that background against which worlds emerge but which remains partially unintelligible, unavailable as material ready-to-hand. On one hand the material provenance of the buttonhook signals a shorthand relation of human extractive industries to the earth they disrupt and transform – invoking Heidegger's concept of *Gestell* or 'standing reserve' – but its near-exhaustion, its failure or refusal to preserve its objecthood and instead to slowly revert to a mineral state, calls attention to the mystery of things when considered as actants rather than simply objects ready-to-hand. Jane Bennett shows how the concept of the actant distributes agency 'across a wider range of ontological types' and finds expression in the medieval legal concept of *deodand* ('that which falls to God'). The deodand is material existing between the status of human and thing – an object causing accidental death such as a carriage – 'surrendered to the crown to be used (or sold) to compensate for the harm done' (Bennett, 2010, 9). The buttonhook, like several other objects in the hovel of *Ill Seen Ill Said*, can be thought of as an expression of the vitality of material formations, a dominant theme in recent Actor Network Theory. Along with other objects in the hovel, it expresses what Bill Brown has called a material unconscious in literary texts – 'whereby the history in things, however unacknowledged by the text, seems to overdetermine their textual presence' (Brown, 2016, 238; see also Brown, 1997). Beckett's objects are antique, decayed, archaic, belonging to an economy preceding modern production. However as focal points of Beckett's narrative, these objects play out a variation of the 'it'-narrative or novel of circulation that gained enormous popularity in the eighteenth century, such as *Golden Spy* by Charles Gildon (1709) and Tobias Smollett's *The History and Adventures of an Atom* (1769) (Bates, 2017, 7; Blackwell, 2014). This material investment complements the influence upon Beckett of eighteenth-century authors such as George Berkeley, Alexander Pope, and Samuel Johnson (see Smith, 2002).

The few other objects given narrative attention also direct their volitional potential towards the earth in a series of subtle mineralogical and evulsive images. Amidst the wooden objects, such as the pallet and the rafters, the chair 'exudes its solitude', asserting its volitional capacity as an actant or its ability to recede from objecthood, 'For want of a fellow-table' (62). An antique coffer appears 'suddenly', but it is the metal utensil, the woman's spoon, and her bowl that unite in the central action. She eats 'in a twin motion full of grace' (echoing here the opening of the *Ave Maria*) following a period of frozen immobility, another gesture of the 'Memnon pose' (62). Later the narrative eye views the room's clock: 'Close-up of a dial. Nothing else. White disc divided in minutes' (69). The clock with 'No figure' and 'No tick' – a variant on Clov's 'No more sugar plums!' 'No more painkillers!' – moves in 'fits and starts', recalling the 'saltatoriality' of light in 'Long Observation of the Ray'. The clock is seen 'pointing east', with the single hand at three: 'Having thus covered after its fashion assuming the instrument plumb the first quarter of its latest hour' (69). The erratic jumpiness of the single hand mimics the action of a compass in its measure of the earth's magnetic field, but points east rather than north, the direction in which the woman moves to pass the standing stones. By describing the fixture of the clock as plumb, the narrator links the clock to the earth, not merely in its upright position on the wall, but etymologically: the term plumb derives from the early use of lead (*plumbum*) on a string to indicate a vertical line – just as earlier snow is described as falling 'plumb through the still air' (61) and the woman's closed eye 'plumbs its dark' (65). Silver is often extracted from ores containing lead – a metallurgic link back to the woman's buttonhook.

Such images pertain not only to the objects in the room, but also to the actions of seeing and moving. As she remembers a moment or figure from her barren past the woman's gaze is '[r]iveted to some detail of the desert the eye fills with tears' (51). The utility and strength of metal rivets derives from the 'tail' being punched hard enough to deform into a second head, allowing them to carry tension loads and shear loads perpendicular to the rivet's shaft. In this sense, the woman's eye fixes upon a memory and gazes out indifferently upon objects in her field of vision. As a riveting action these dimensions are bound together in her gaze, even if their forces tend in different directions. Soon after the buttonhook is introduced, the disembodied eye observes the woman's hovel. The eye's vision is blurred and confused, and time variously dilates and accelerates. However the eye's act of seeing is given the same metallurgic image as the woman's: 'The eye rivets the bare window' (53). In this case the bond is not secure and the forceful act of riveting only serves to detach observation from the wider field of vision. The narrator assesses this scene of confusion and pronounces 'If only she could be pure figment. Unalloyed' (53), likening the woman's status to pure metal, forbidding admixture of any other element to produce an alloy or amalgam. Pure metals rarely occur in nature: unalloyed metal is the product of considerable processes of smelting, electrolysis, or other methods. The narrator's desire for 'pure figment' is as likely as a desire for pure platinum or pure copper.

A Sharp Nose for Detritus

The crepuscular world of *Ill Seen Ill Said* is remarkably free of detritus and waste. White stones are strewn over the landscape, and the woman's hut shows signs of decay in its worn flagstone and humble furnishings, but the characteristic decay of objects in Beckett's prose and drama – bicycles, crutches, sticks, boots – is scaled down to the woman's greatcoat which, like the hovel's curtains – one of which may be the deceased husband's black greatcoat (70) – shows little sign of decay. Little is made of her physical frailties compared to younger compatriots in the Beckett country such as Watt, Hamm, Clov, Estragon, and Vladimir. Yet the passage of time, the framing and partial convergence of a human habitus with geological and celestial timescales, is at the centre of the woman's negotiations with her world. Rather than ill-seeing, the location of the story's detritus is in the ill-saying: the narrative is strewn with partial references to a range of canonical literary texts as well as a disarming number of Beckett's own works, glinting in the half-light just as the chalky ground and white stones reflect the moonlight. It is as though *Ill Seen Ill Said* itself is a remnant slate – a tile but also a writing surface – 'brought from a ruined mansion' (67) of Beckett's oeuvre and his store of literary and cultural references. It as though this text is to Beckett's cultural patrimony as the woman's hovel is to the Irish big house and its literary tradition.

The hovel, as an 'abode of things', is a storehouse for literary reference and material documents, oscillating between repository and garbage dump. The woman keeps 'a still shadowy album' under her pillow or 'deep in some recess', her 'old fingers fumbl[ing] through the pages' (50). Another marker of this documentary index is the 'coffer', located 'after long nocturnal search' and found to be almost empty:

> Nothing. Save in the end in a cranny of dust a scrap of paper. Jagged along one edge as if torn from a diary. On its yellowed face in barely legible ink two letters followed by a number. Tu 17. Or Th. Tu or Th 17. Otherwise blank. Otherwise empty. (64)

The coffer, containing barely more than the dust of a once-living diary, recalls the dust to which all deceased humans return upon burial. This association dwells in Beckett's vocabulary, where 'coffer' shares the same linguistic root as 'coffin' – from the Greek κόφινος (basket) loaned to become the Latin *cophinus*. The coffer as pseudo-coffin also performs a similar function to the Celtic *kistvaen*, a box-like burial chamber made of stone and often buried beneath a *tumulus*. The manuscript fragment it contains comprises an ambiguous textual remnant: the Anglo-Saxon weekday names produce two abbreviations too similar to distinguish in the damaged document, a situation from which Old Irish weekday names are immune (although not so for Romance languages if Tuesday and Wednesday are the days at issue, or indeed modern Irish if Sunday [*An Domhnach*] and Thursday [*An Déardaoin*] are the two days in question). The coffer is also the scene of the woman's prayers – quickly emended to 'grovellings' by the narrator – a function it shares with the chair and 'the edge of the pastures with her head on the stones' (65).

These associations between death, internment, storage, and textuality extend to the trapdoor discovered in the floor's '[e]bony boards' soon after 'the coffer fiasco' (66). The narrating eye considers the risk of 'another rebuff', that is, the disappointment of finding an empty vault. This cites two markers of Christian salvation: Lazarus vacating his vault, and Christ's resurrection from the tomb belonging to Joseph of Arimathea. Combined with the stars and moon, the presence of this trapdoor recalls the twin myths of egress from the cylinder in

The Lost Ones: a secret passage 'leading in the words of the poet to nature's sanctuaries', and 'a trapdoor hidden in the hub of the ceiling giving access to a flue at the end of which the sun and other stars would still be shining' (*TFN* 105). *Le dépeupleur* makes clearer than the English text that the poet is Lamartine and his words are from the poem 'Le Vallon' (Caselli, 2005, 195; see also Long, 2000, 154). *Mal vu mal dit* also concludes its reference to the trapdoor with the word *étoiles* (stars), the same word that concludes each canticle of Dante's *Commedia*. Beckett has the woman consider the stars and the earthworks beneath her in a Dantescan frame, enhanced by the circular zoning within which her shelter is situated – a topography that also recalls *The Lost Ones*.

Each repository contains its own textual remnants: the coffer with its scrap of diary suggests how events transform into fragments of a past life; and the trapdoor functions as an entry point to Beckett's own texts and his most significant intertextual influences. A later inventory of objects in the hovel returns to the scene of writing and reading in another repositorial space, 'possibly a hutch' (74). The scene concludes: 'The sheet. Between tips of trembling fingers. In two. Four. Eight. Old frantic fingers. Not paper any more. Each eighth apart. In two. Four. Finish with the knife. Hack into shreds. Down the plughole. On to the next. White. Quick blacken' (75). This sheet, contents unknown and condemned to serial defacement, appears at a point in the narrative where dense intertextual allusion and etymological play draw attention to the porosity of texts. It also recalls how some of the most significant archaeological discoveries have occurred at ancient garbage sites, such as the Oxyrhynchus papyri in Egypt: an enormous cache of textual material in Latin and Arabic (with a few texts composed in Aramaic, Hebrew, Coptic, Syriac, and Pahlavi) discovered by Bernard Grenfell and Arthur Hunt in excavations between 1896 and 1907. Once reconstructed from small papyri fragments, these were found to contain works by Sappho, Aristotle, Menander, and Euclid, among others, as well as biblical and apocryphal texts, and even larger multitudes of tax assessments, court documents, and other civil texts.

The condition of textual fragments found in the hovel indicates a lost world, exhumed and partially reconstructed by the archaeology of interpretation. The association of textual fragments with burial also recalls the Jewish of גניזה (*genizah*, 'to hide', 'to put away'): a structure in which disintegrating Hebrew religious texts, or indeed any text containing the divine name are stored, prior to their interment in a burial service. The narrator, not content with this diminished textual condition, looks ahead to a 'great leap into what brief future remains' (75) to imagine the collapse of the house and '[a]ll that fond trash' (76) found within it. This condition of habitus reduced to household trash also entails spent

emotion. When the coats and buttonhook are removed for good, a correspond-
ing series of sighs peter out to nothing: 'And been hove the sigh no more than
that. Sigh upon sigh till all sighed quite away' (76). This domestic archaeological site draws attention to the play on the word 'till' as time ('until') and
turning the soil ('to till'), but the double meaning in the word 'hove' brings the
woman's abode and its decrepit contents into focus. Her sighs are reported
retrospectively – *hove* as the past tense of *heave* – but the word also deliberates
on her small world: it derives from the Old English *hofian* ('to receive into one's
house'), itself from the Proto-Germanic *hufōną* ('to house or lodge') and *hufą*
('hill, farm, dwelling'), and is cognate with *hovel*, the word used to describe the
woman's dwelling. Thus hospitality, shelter, and agriculture are united in this
word's etymology, providing a record of how meaning and usage, and languages themselves, are eventually cast aside, to be redeemed as 'all that fond
trash' by the attentive reader.

Ill Seen Ill Said comprises a rich rubbish dump of fragmented literary
references. Beckett famously rejected what he called the 'loutishness of learning' evident in his earlier work, especially *Dream of Fair to Middling Women*
and *Murphy*, instead submerging literary reference beneath the text surface, like
so many fossils awaiting discovery. The density of intertextual reference in *Ill
Seen Ill Said* is notable for its return to the encyclopaedic style of his earlier
work, where this late style casts a critical eye over his career. This also imbues
intertextual reference with a certain irony, rewarding the assiduous reader for
memory work and keen perception, and demonstrating that allusion is most
effective when its motivations are rich and multi-layered rather than simply
ends in themselves. This is the kind of 'auto-speliology' that might have
occupied Beckett earlier in his career, but here it provides the reader with
substantial stratigraphic material: the sum of Beckett's texts to which reference
is made in *Ill Seen Ill Said*; and the hermeneutic nuance scholars can bring to
them by virtue of an enhanced understanding of his reading, his composition
practices, and his textual genesis newly illuminated in the 'documentary turn'.
As Marjorie Perloff has suggested, this late-career resurgence of allusion may
also be tied to the process of writing first in French and then transforming the
text into English: 'Increasingly, in the prose of his old age, the Anglo-Irish
schoolroom of the writer's youth is coming in by the back door – which is to say,
the door of translation' (Perloff, 1990, 163).

The early narrative establishes the narrator's power over the woman merely in
the act of perceiving her visually, recalling Beckett's nod to George Berkeley's
tenet in *The Principles of Human Knowledge*: *esse est percipi* ('To be is to be
seen'). This ontospeliological keynote underwrites a series of allusions and self-
citations. The narrator notes the woman's absences – 'Times when she is gone'

(51) – although the reader is left to determine whether or not the woman's absence is due to the narrating eye's errancy. The text provides potential clues: 'At crocus time it would be making for the distant tomb. To have that on the imagination!' (56). The association between crocus and internment is familiar from *How It Is*: 'I see a crocus in a pot in an area in a basement' (*H* 15). A perennial favourite in Beckett's arboreal repertoire, it appears in such early texts as *The End* – 'manured' and 'watered' with limited success by the narrator in his basement (*TE* 41-43) – and *Watt*, when Arsene makes reference to its early bloom along with the larch 'and the pastures red with uneaten sheep's placentas' (*W* 38). This latter image forges another link with *Ill Seen Ill Said*, its sheep grazing the pastures beyond the zone of stones, where the 'lamb goes no further' than the tomb (64). Just as the coffer, empty of all except a handful of paper fragments, recalls the resurrection, so here the lamb and the tomb rehearse Christian imagery.

This early section of the narrative initiates two conceits that comprise stratigraphic layers across Beckett's career: the use of biblical imagery and the vocabulary of Romanticism. The woman is '[n]o longer anywhere to be seen [. . .] by the eye of flesh nor by the other' (51). The 'eye of flesh' appears in *The Expelled*, *The Lost Ones*, and elsewhere, sustaining a nod to Job 10:4 in the King James Bible: 'Hast thou eyes of flesh? Or seest thou as man seeth?' It also echoes the 'vile jelly' (73) of *King Lear* arising also in *Company*. The following paragraph speaks of the tearful eye '[r]iveted to some detail of the desert [. . .] Imagination at wit's end spreads its sad wings' (51). The invocation of the desert bears any number of theological analogies – the wandering Israelites in the Sinai following the Exodus from Egypt, Christ's temptation, the early Christian Anchorites – but also the truncated statue of Ozymandias, its feet emerging from the desert sands. By invoking the imagination in an avian metaphor (and deploying the pathetic fallacy of 'sad wings'), Shelley's 'To a Sky-Lark' and John Keats's 'Ode to a Nightingale' linger nearby, as well as making reference to the zoomorphic form of the dove in the third Person of the Christian Trinity. Beckett's vocabulary reinforces this late-career homage to Romanticism, where a moonlight walk breaks the 'monotony' and yields '[t]he limp grass strangely rigid under the weight of the rime' (66), bringing Anglophone boats to the shore of Coleridge's Ancient Mariner. The woman's 'scalding' tears (57) also trace a direct line to Krapp, 'Scalding the eyes out of me reading *Effie* [*Effi Briest*] again, a page a day' (*K* 11), to Dan Rooney's request for Maddy to read him the same novel in *All That Fall* (*ATF* 21), and ultimately to Beckett's own repeated reading: first with his tubercular cousin Peggy Sinclair in 1929 down to his fourth reading reported in a letter to Barney Rosset of 26 May 1956 (*LII* 621; see also Van Hulle and Nixon, 2013, 97–9).

The conjugation of biblical allusion with Romantic vocabulary reaches a geomorphic zenith in a sequence conflating the fallen house with the hill of Golgotha:

> First the curtains gone without loss of dark. Sweet foretaste of the joy at journey's end. Second after long hesitation no trace of the fallen where they fell. No trace of all the ado. Alone on the one hand the rods alone. A little bent. And alone on the other most alone the nail. Unimpaired. All set to serve again. Like unto its glorious ancestors. At the place of the skull. One April afternoon. Deposition alone. (76)

Contrary to the claim 'No trace of all the ado' (echoes of Shakespeare) intertextual traces are to be found throughout this passage: the Christian drama of the *felix culpa* in 'fallen', and the word 'joy', an index of Romanticism, which takes a concentrated form in *Worstward Ho*. The nail serving as a curtain hook cites the objects of the crucifixion but also nods to the 'hammer and three nails' embedded in the names of *Endgame*'s four characters. The small hill of Golgotha ('the place of the skull) – given in Matthew and Mark as Κρανίου Τόπος and rendered in Latin as *Calvariae topos* – also marks the moment of Beckett's own nativity on Good Friday, 13 April 1906. It neatly captures Pozzo's lament in *Waiting for Godot* that we are all 'born astride the grave' (*G* 86). Once the site of a quarry, Golgotha also echoes the clinking of the hammers at Beckett's birth.

As the woman sits before the stones, 'Head haught now she gazes into emptiness' (63–4), her stature recalls that seen in *Ping*, 'Head haught eyes light blue' (*TFN* 123). Her stature '[f]rom the waist up' when 'seen from behind' is that of '[t]runk black rectangle' (58), which recalls the '[l]ittle body little block' of *Lessness* (*TFN* 129–32) and looks ahead to the 'old man hindtrunk' of *Worstward Ho* (*WH* 101). The clock within the woman's hovel is figured as a kind of compass, '[e]ver regaining north' (69), just as the 'woman vanquished' in *The Lost Ones* 'is the north' (*TFN* 118). The narrator's powers of vision retreat from the scene, '[n]ot possible any longer except as figment' (59), which recalls the felicitous final sentence of *Lessness*, 'Figment dawn dispeller of figments and the other called dusk' (*TFN* 132) – the 'ruins true refuge' permeating *Lessness* also find an afterlife in the woman's hovel. The crepuscular evening in *Ill Seen Ill Said* is an undecidable choice between victory and loss – 'On the one hand embers. On the other ashes' (65) – recalling Beckett's play *Embers* in its meditation on loss, and the physical loss of Murphy's ashes, not to mention the 'ash grey' of the 'little body' in *Lessness*. The problem of identifying the real and its contrary – 'That old tandem' (65) – recalls the fondly recollected tandem in *Endgame* on which Nagg and Nell lost their shanks in the

Ardennes. The final paragraph of the narrative begins with a foreshadowing of Beckett's final text, the poem 'What Is the Word': 'Decision no sooner reached or rather long after than what is the wrong word?' (77–8) – a proleptic '[f]arewell to farewell' (78). The next sentence looks back – 'For the last time at last for to end yet again what the wrong word?' (78) – where the verbless final phrase emphasizes the reverberating name of *Watt*, and 'for to end yet again' restates the title of the seventh *Fizzle* (*TFN* 151–3). Beckett's obsessive circling back on certain terms and phrases makes such echoes inevitable. These examples mostly comprise straightforward allusion, but Beckett also installs eroded references in his texts less obtrusively, keeping readers and scholars alive to hidden nuggets in the midden of language.

Beckett's eye for language also shows how its erosion over time gives new life to archaisms. The presence of the word 'till' in the first paragraph (45) looks ahead to its etymologically rich usage in *Worstward Ho*. A blazon identifies several of the woman's features in archaic terms: her hair is '[r]igidly horrent' (59), that is, standing on end (the word's etymology also allows for the reaction to horror, thus the modern 'abhorrent'); her palms are held up and then 'fall back pronating as they go' (60), turned inwards and downwards; her eyes are 'washen blue' (65), from the Old English *wascen* meaning 'clean' in its adjectival form; the '[o]pe eye' (74) of the narrator draws on Middle English usage, where the word functions adjectivally, or else as a transitive or intransitive verb, each of which usages bears directly on how the relation between the eye and the subjectivity opening it are understood (as does its mood, whether indicative or imperative); the woman's eye is further described in a condition of 'slumbrous collapsion' (75), the 'uncommon common noun' an archaic Latinate usage; and this process of observation is described using the French verb form *scruter* (to inspect), 'To scrute together with the inscrutable face' (75). Observation runs up against its limits, both of perception and diagnosis, where the forensic efforts of the viewing subject finds, as Murphy with Mr Endon, a dark mirror reflecting nothing back but the void of affect.

4 Wordly Corrasions in *Worstward Ho*

Worstward Ho is a text of last words: it abrades the last word of character, narrative, and language as it approaches the condition of silence. Comprised of a small group of relatively simple words that proliferate, break apart, and form new grammar and syntax, it casts its ambitions across the production of language and literature. Its philological awareness forms a micro-history of the rise and eclipse of languages – a linguistic equivalent of geological time, where rock layers form, continents drift, and seismic change ruptures the living surface of the world. By negotiating the terms and structures of literary world-making (and unmaking) the text also creates new modes of reference, both to the literary canon and to Beckett's own works. Its appearance belies its status as one of the most difficult prose texts in all of literature: Beckett conceded that it was 'untranslatable' (Knowlson, 1996, 684–5), although Erika Tophoven translated the text into German as *Aufs Schlimmste zu* (1989), Edith Fournier translated it into French as *Cap au pire* (1991), and Kaku Nagashima produced a highly regarded Japanese translation, *Iza saiaku no hō e* (1999). In a letter of 23 August 1982 Beckett reported to Barbara Bray mid-composition that *Worstward Ho* was a text he couldn't face (*LIV* 591), and in a letter of 19 May 1983 to André Bernold he stated 'Je crois que *Worstward Ho* m'a achevé' ('I think that *Worstward Ho* has finished me off') (*LIV* 610). In its approach to the endpoint of thought and language, *Worstward Ho* has been compared to Dante's *Commedia*, manifesting a 'godless comedy' that concludes in a strikingly different 'vision of eternity' (Hisgen, 1998, 534). Yet Beckett's eschatology was directed not to the heavens but firmly earthward. On completing the text he declared to Kay Boyle in a letter of 16 December 1983: 'Seem to have succeeded at last in writing myself into the ground' (quoted in Hisgen, 1998, 27).

Beckett creates this earthy epic quality in *Worstward Ho* by drawing on a career of literary technique and philology, refined in a series of archaeological, geomorphological, and geological tropes. The linguistic mechanisms by which concepts are formed and dissolved and re-formed perform a kind of literary cosmogony, a creation of a universe in language, but one subject to processes of geological erosion and agricultural accretion. This is evident in the way simple words are distended to create new modes of measuring the emergent narrative world, where individual words slide across grammatical categories to create new ways of thinking about movement, consciousness, light, narration, identity, memory, and embodiment. These folds of language and image bring a narrative into being that equally seeks to approach the condition of its own extinction, its 'nohow on'. *Worstward Ho* creates a language that is *sui generis* but that also manufactures its own fossils, the traces of its linguistic and literary heritage. It grapples with the first principles of literary narrative in two related ways: firstly in philology, where the etymologies of particular words exhibit a persistent return to the language of land, farming, and terrain, revealing a close relationship with writing and literature; and secondly, in reference to texts across Beckett's oeuvre as well as across the literary canon, again revealing a fascination with geology, landforms, and masonry. The sedimentation of language and literary reference in *Worstward Ho* becomes the narrative's geo-textual record.

Earthworks: Philology

The first paragraph of the text establishes the event of narrative creation as well as its logic: 'On. Say on. Be said on. Somehow on. Till nohow on. Said nohow on' (*WH* 81). These initial fourteen words across six sentences demonstrate dense lexical repetition, variety and ambiguity in verbal tense, aspect, and modality, and invention in the critical neologism 'nohow'. The staccato rhythm of short sentences, each ending with the word 'on', comprises the groundwork for the expanding and contracting terrain of the narrative. This neat sequence, strung across the page and framed by abundant space, draws attention to the physical distribution of the text, as though the rows of words have been planted there for later harvesting. The word 'till' refers to a hypothetical future moment at which 'nohow on' is reached and the narrative desists, but it also invokes the tillage of language on the field of the page, as well as the tillage of Beckett's oeuvre for previous incarnations of this wordplay, from *More Pricks Than Kicks* to *Ill Seen Ill Said*. This usage plays on the classical trope of the page-as-vineyard, a site of cultivation and harvesting, which, as Pliny noted, is captured in the way the Latin word *pagina* also refers to rows of vines: 'The lines on the page were thus the threads of a trellis that supported the vines' (Illich, 1993, 57).

This textual cultivation persists in the sense of the narrator's tillage of the verbal field – 'Say for be said. Missaid. Say for be missaid' (81) – and in the process of conceptual refinement in which phrases and definitions are substituted in the pursuit of the 'best worse'. Adriaan van der Weel notes that the first two establishing paragraphs, absent from the two manuscript drafts and the first typescript and appearing belatedly in the second typescript (1998, 23), reflect a 'break in style' with the rest of *Worstward Ho*. During the composition process, Beckett referred to the text as 'Better worse', as he records in a letter to Lawrence Shainberg of 7 January 1983 (*LIV* 604). Once the dimensions of its cosmos have been sufficiently installed, processes of linguistic and conceptual reduction dominate the second half of *Worstward Ho*. The aspiration to reduce allusive and figurative potential in the narrative is directed by speech acts of 'worsening' and lessening', but even these expressions are unable to resist the potential for lyricism: 'To last unlessenable least how loath to leasten' (96). The word 'lessen' bears echoes of the etymology of reading, from the German verb *lesen* and back to the Latin verb *legere*, both of which also refer to gathering bundles or harvests: to read is to bundle alphabetic units into syllabic harvests on the page (Illich, 1993, 58). These agricultural echoes – each tied to reading, literacy, and the production of literature – neatly combine the grounding gestures of narrative cultivation with the matter of tillage, the strings and clods of words on the page. These protean acts of narration emulate classical pastoral genres of poetry such as Hesiod's *Works and Days* and Virgil's *Eclogues* and *Georgics*. But in Beckett's text, the founding act initiates a process of erosion, where narrative cultivates the possibility of approaching its ultimate diminishment, and, to adapt Hamm's vision of complete human solitude in *Endgame*, where narrative agency becomes the last piece of grit to be blown from the vast steppe (*E* 23–4).

Early in the narrative, the physical features of the space are described in geological terms: 'Say a grot in that void. A gulf' (86). The Latinate word *grotto* ('of a cave') derives from Old French, as does *gulf*, but the Anglo-Saxon word *grot*, now obsolete, refers to a fragment or particle (Hamm's grit on the steppe). In its Old Norse form *grot* also has the meaning of weeping or lamentation. The Latinate noun *void* can mean 'unproductive land', and as a verb it can signify the erosive action of a river or the act of excavation. The void in *Worstward Ho* contains the three shades: the man and child, the woman, and the seeing head. As the space expands and narrows it is associated with the Latinate *vast* deployed as a qualifying noun: 'In that narrow void vasts of void apart' (92). This word also bears geological residues, where *vast* describes open uncultivated land, this usage having evolved into the word *waste* (thus *The Waste Land*). The space occupied by the first shade of man and child becomes a *rift* (96), the word recurring with the Middle English archaisms *atwain* (to be composed of two parts; to be riven) and *atween* (between): 'Since atwain. Two once so one. From now rift a vast. Vast of void atween' (100). The Germanic *rift* describes ploughed farmlands, and is a key term in Martin Heidegger's essay 'The Origin of the Work of Art', where the translator's note suggests direct implications for the sedimentation of language in *Worstward Ho*:

> In German *der Riss* is a crack, tear, laceration, cleft, or rift; but it is also a plan or design in drawing. The verb *reissen* from which it derives is cognate with the English word *writing*. *Der Riss* is incised or inscribed as a rune or letter. Heidegger here employs a series of words (*Abriss*, *Aufriss*, *Umriss*, and especially *Grundriss*) to suggest that the rift of world and earth releases a sketch, outline, profile, blueprint, or ground plan. (1993, 188)

The confluence of philology, geology, and farming in the word *rift* consolidates its place as a pivotal word in Beckett's text, especially in its reflexive sense of compositional space and narrative space as cognate dimensions of textuality. *Rift* also refers to the way protruding rocks create pools of river water, and is thus intimately related to corrasion, or the process of mineral erosion by water. In its Old English form, *rift* also bore the now-obsolete meaning 'to cover', or 'arch over', thus providing an elegant bond with images of archaeology and masonry in *Worstward Ho*.

Worstward Ho's topography operates by decree of measure and proportion. Measurements of light are dominated by Latinate words: 'Dim light source unknown. Know minimum. Know nothing no. Too much to hope. At most mere minimum. Meremost minimum' (82). This unknown light source recalls the 'no visible source' of light in the rotunda in *Imagination Dead Imagine*, another space where a stone structure (a vault) mimics the shape of the skull, as well as the 'hidden sources' of light in *The Lost Ones*, with its 'luminous [...] stridulence' and 'vibration' emanating from an unseen 'commutator' (*ATF* 112–13). Instead of the narrator attempting (and failing) to understand a system with hidden or unknowable controls by way of a Latinate vocabulary – a narrative strategy amply illustrated in *The Lost Ones* and iterated elsewhere in Beckett's oeuvre – the narrator of *Worstward Ho* sets his sights more modestly. The hope to 'know nothing' is too ambitious in its absoluteness (it is 'too much' to ask for 'nothing') and instead embarks on an approach to nothing, 'Meremost minimum', in which the language of excess (most) and diminishment (mere, minimum) combines to produce a superlative expression, noting also that the Germanic word *mere* is yet another term for a land boundary or body of water. Similarly, the pursuit of 'worseness' paradoxically makes worse better and least best (once 'naught', another Anglo-Saxon word, is ruled out).

> Worse less. By no stretch more. Worse for want of better less. Less best. No. Naught best. Best worse. No. Not best worse. Naught not best worse. Less best worse. No. Least. Least best worse. Least never to be naught. Never to naught be brought. Never by naught be nulled. Unnullable least. Say that best worse. With leastening words say least best worse. For want of worser worst. Unlessenable least best worse. (94–5)

For the reader, 'better' is easily confused with 'worse' in the pursuit of the least possible, the 'unlessenable least best worse'. This apparent contradiction makes sense within the narrative's economy, where the pursuit of the 'worst' is to find the 'best worse', and this is found in the concept of the 'unlessenable least', the closest that presence can approach pure absence. The passage works through a process, evident in words such as 'worse' or 'leastening', to arrive at a concept not pure in itself, but insurmountable within the necessity of presence demanded by the text's narrator.

Wherefore the strong bonds of agriculture, geology, and etymology in the vocabulary of *Worstward Ho*? Beckett's oeuvre offers precedence for matters of gardening: Mr Graves in *Watt*, whose name resonates with the earthy matter of burial; and the quincunxial forms of the tunnels in *The Lost Ones* that draw on Thomas Browne's *Garden of Cyrus*. Instances of quarrying and earthworks also saturate Beckett's texts: the stonecutters' hammers echoing in *Watt*, *Malone Dies*, and *First Love*; the mud of *How It Is*; Winnie's earthy internment in *Happy Days*; and the cromlech of Glen Druid looming behind the standing stones of *Ill Seen Ill Said* (Brater, 1994, 124–6).

These kinds of excavations *in* Beckett's texts prompt questions concerning the excavation *of* his texts, especially the role of manuscripts and other archival materials that have radically transformed the understanding of his work in recent decades. Chris Ackerley has mined the 'geology of the imagination' in the *Watt* notebooks, showing how layers of mind and mud are manifested in the visible stratifications of the published text, especially in the Addenda 'fossils' (Ackerley, 2004 and 1993). Gerry Dukes has argued that Beckett's trilogy of novels served as a kind of quarry for much of the prose to follow, and Mark Nixon states: 'there is much evidence to suggest that Beckett perceived the writing process as a site of excavation, and geological terminology is scattered throughout manuscript material' (Dukes, 1993, 197–24; Nixon, 2006). The 'Sottisier' Notebook contains notes towards *Worstward Ho* – a reference to Charles Kingsley's text as a source for its title and relevant quotations from *King Lear* – as well as notes towards associated texts such as 'Ceiling' and 'The Way'. Adriaan van der Weel considers both of these texts to be *paralipomena* by virtue of the proximity of theme and composition (1998, 291). This notebook marks something of a return to this form of note-taking after the flurry of 'note-snatching' in the 1930s subsided (Van Hulle and Nixon, 2013, 14), Beckett having preferred in the interim to submerge literary allusions beneath the text surface. *Worstward Ho* brings to fruition a lifelong process in its vocabulary of digging, cultivating, and writing, where '[t]he geological terminology harnessed by Beckett, the notion of excavation and mining, serves to merge the textual and existential layers' (Nixon, 2006).

'Bits of Pipe': Archaeology

Worstward Ho invites various kinds of hermeneutic earthworks, where the reader is invited to dig, to follow linguistic and allusive veins in search of hidden nuggets or reefs, and to construct the foundations of textual understanding on clearly defined strata. The challenge to identify potential intertextual influences is amplified by the text's experiments with basic linguistic functions as well as its concentrated and highly reticulated vocabulary. Beckett draws upon the fund of concepts and images from his prose texts and drama, framing *Worstward Ho* as a subtle commentary on and culmination of several lifelong preoccupations. Ruud Hisgen has even called it Beckett's *caput mortuum* or *tête morte*, adapting a term for alchemical residua to signify the essence and epitome of an entire writing career defined by the aspiration to decline and decay (1998, 361). Operations of light and shade in Beckett's corpus as early as *Murphy* have received comprehensive critical treatment (see Knowlson, 1972), with implications for the 'dim' and the 'shades' of *Worstward Ho* (Shaw, 2012, 225–7). The narrative ambiguity concerning the description and control of light bears strong echoes of the function of light in such prose texts as *All Strange Away*, *Imagination Dead Imagine*, and *The Lost Ones*. The '[c]lenched staring eyes' (83) that come to 'prey' on the emergent shades (86, 98–9) mirror the 'eye of prey' in *Imagination Dead Imagine* (*ATF* 89) and reflect the many staring eyes in Beckett's oeuvre such as the sudden meeting of eyes between E and the awakened O in *Film*: 'The staring eyes. Dimly seen. By the staring eyes' (*WH* 91). Despite its pared vocabulary, *Worstward Ho* demonstrates Beckett's fascination with archaisms and neologisms: the presence of 'atwain' and 'atween' (100) as well as the pseudo-Elizabethan exclamation 'A pox on bad' (89) recall proximate occurrences as 'horrent' (59) and 'collapsion' (75) in *Ill Seen Ill Said*. The narrator's exclamation at the prospect of 'Meaning!' (88) echoes Hamm's fear in *Endgame* that he and Clov might be 'beginning to … to … mean something' (*E* 22). The conflation of bone and stone in *Worstward Ho* is aided by intertextual echoes: the 'near true ring' of the skull (90) recalls the 'ring of bone' in *Imagination Dead Imagine* (*ATF* 87), merging the whitened vault in which the living bodies are interred with the cranial vault of human imagination. The cromlech and the gravestone visited by the old woman in *Ill Seen Ill Said* resonate with 'that old graveyard' visited by the second shade, the old woman (*WH* 102). Gravestones scatter throughout Beckett's oeuvre as well as in unpublished manuscript material – Quin sees the letters of his name 'flee' from his imagined gravestone in the first *Watt* manuscript notebook – and gather in *Worstward Ho* to signify how writing is intimately joined to the displacement of earth and the installation of memorializing granite and sandstone, where these remnants frame textual production as the fashioning of a posthumous monument, an 'Ozymandias of the page' (Byron, 2017, 130). To be born astride the grave is also to recognize the imperatives of earthworks within a human lifespan, whether the craft of Yorrick or the art of literary composition.

The compound origins of the text's title are well known and include John Webster and Thomas Dekker's Jacobean comedy *Westward Hoe* (1607), Charles Kingsley's historical novel *Westward Ho!* (1855), and Viola's line in Shakespeare's *Twelfth Night* (1602), 'Then westward ho!' (Act 3, Scene 1, 134). In a letter of 16 December 1982 Beckett tells Barney Rosset directly of the Kingsley connection (*LIV* 597). The 'Sottisier' Notebook provides direct evidence of intertextual influence in such quotations from *King Lear* as: 'The worst is not / So long as we can say, "This is the worst"' (Act 4, Scene 1, 28–9) (Knowlson, 1996, 674; Weller, 2005, 191; Chattopadhyay, 2012, 74), and 'The worst returns to laughter' (Act 4, Scene 1, 6) which resonates in the first poem of the *Mirlitonnades*: 'en face / le pire / jusqu'à ce / qu'il fasse rire' (*CP* 210). John Pilling dilates the Shakespearean catalogue echoing in the title, linking it to Othello's apotropaic formula for the word 'death' in his phrase the 'worst of words' and Julius Caesar's 'Give the word, Ho!' (Pilling, 1986, 25–6). Claudio's speech in *Measure for Measure* also resonates, where the journey towards death as 'worse than worst' (Act 3, Scene 1, 126) deploys the familiar trope of the western voyage towards death, evident in John Donne's poetry and elsewhere (Hisgen, 1998, 525). Beckett's acute attention to philology is evident in the presence of faux archaisms ('pox', 'atween', 'grot') and the careful distribution of Anglo-Saxon vocabulary ('whither', 'whence', 'thither', 'thence'). This vocabulary is one of orientation, direction, and relative position in time or space, whereas Beckett's Latinate usages in *The Lost Ones* and elsewhere attempt (and fail at) quantification, precise measurement, and control. Densely poetic lines erupt at pivotal points in the narrative – 'Never to naught be brought. Never by naught be nulled' (95); 'To last unlessenable least how loath to leasten' (96) – and exhibitions of linguistic dexterity abound, such as the astonishing but perfectly intelligible phrase: 'Whenever said said said missaid' (97).

This intimate coordination of literary history and linguistic experimentation performs an homage to Beckett's native language, testimony to its eclectic fertility. It is as though English in all of its complex rootedness is the soil giving rise to the strange vegetation of literary expression. Remnant Romantic vocabulary persists in the narrator's registration of sufficient mind and language: 'Just enough still to joy. Joy!' (93). This key word transects the Romantic corpus, from Friedrich Schiller's 'An die Freude' ('Ode to Joy') to John Keats's *Endymion*, with its opening line, 'A thing of beauty is a joy for ever', and spanning all the major poets in German and English (Potkay, 2007). Appropriately, 'joy' suggests further literary creativity in *Worstward Ho*, appealing to that quintessentially Romantic organ of the mind: the imagination. Romantic imagery also lurks in the *rifts* and *vasts* of the text: Coleridge's 'Kubla Khan' shifts its focus from the Khan's 'pleasure dome' to the 'deep romantic chasm' forged by the river Alph (Coleridge, 1985, 102–4). This river, coursing through 'caverns measureless to man' (l. 4), leads to a vision within a vision, producing pools 'mid these dancing rocks' (l. 23) – the very definition of a *rift*. The work of water and ice upon rock – 'Huge fragments vaulted like rebounding hail' (l. 21) – produces the effect of corrasion in these mysterious caves, inducing a vision of the 'Abyssinian maid' singing with her dulcimer (1. 40). This vision in turn induces the imaginative vision of the poet's own aery 'dome' as well as his imagined visage of 'flashing eyes' and 'floating hair' (1. 50), a scenario all the more astonishing as a blueprint for Krapp's vision on the Dun Laoghaire jetty. The initial vision of a walled city in Coleridge's poem gives way to hidden caverns, subterranean rivers, the grinding of ice and rock, and the sedimentation of poetic inspiration into future vital bardic utterance. That Coleridge chooses to frame this poetic effort as an aethereal work of architecture, a sunny dome of the air and of the mind, draws it even closer to the 'dome' (or 'no dome') of *Worstward Ho*: the skull that becomes simply foreskull, the 'seat and germ of all' (94), of thought and inspiration, now 'soft' and 'ooze'.

Grotto: Masonry

In a letter of 11 April 1972 to James Knowlson, Beckett called his spare intertextual scaffolding 'bits of pipe' (Knowlson, 1983, 16). *Worstward Ho* calls upon this image as the material setting for its protean narrative: 'Say a pipe in that void. [. . .] Then in that pipe or tube that selfsame dim' (90). The text also engages its own masonry in its attention to such topographical extremities as rifts, vasts, and gulfs. *Grotto* – 'Say a grot in that void. A gulf' (86) – is the etymological source of the word *grotesque*, which in turn describes an artwork found in a grotto, much as the inspired vision within measureless caverns becomes its own artwork in Coleridge's poem. But this image also recalls another literary 'grot', namely Alexander Pope's grotto beneath his Twickenham villa. John Pilling has observed that Beckett includes various quotations from Pope in his letters around the time he begins composition of *Worstward Ho* (Pilling, 2006, 213 and 215). As Pope's Twickenham estate was bisected by the London highway, he had a passageway built under the road to join the Neo-Palladian house with his extensive gardens. Pope's favourite view was from the garden in front of the house, through the grotto to the Thames, where he would see boats suddenly appear and pass. Pope set up a study within his grotto as a refuge from the world: 'The grotto has, in other words, all the signs of an active cognitive ecology, a space of thinking that captured something about how Pope saw his place in the world' (Silver, 2015, 87). This faux archaic assemblage combined architecture and landscape in what Diana Balmori has termed an 'intermediate structure', a category including such structures as hermitages and artificial ruins (Balmori, 1991, 38). 'Pope's grotto, far from appearing "natural" in an anachronistic photographic sense, assembles his stone into striking lines and veins of difference; it cleans up the mess of stones that must have arrived on his porch, fixing them with invisible mechanisms, mortar and clamps, into clean lines and demarcations' (Silver, 2015, 92). Pope had massive urns and several marble statues constructed by stonemasons from Ralph Allen of Bath, as well as several tonnes of rough stone, Plymouth marble, and feldspar slabs from Cornwall. Sir John Sloane gifted Pope two basalt stones from the Giant's Causeway in County Antrim for his grotto irrigated by three separate spring-fed waterfalls (Willson, 1998, 18–20). Pope even installed a piece of marble in the middle of the grotto ceiling acquired from the Grotto of Egeria near Rome. This grotto was established by the legendary Roman philosopher-king Numa and was named for the nymph who became his muse. As the figure responsible for steering Rome from the martial excesses of Romulus, Numa, and by extension, his grotto, came to stand for a kind of civic decorum for Pope (Silver, 2015, 94).

The grotto's combination of design and landscape, *poiesis* and *natura*, is absorbed into the fabric of Beckett's text, whereby writing, tillage, and masonry combine by means of philology. There are important thematic and hermeneutic lessons to draw from Pope's edifice in trying to understand the serial structures arising in the cosmos of *Worstward Ho*. The space contracts from a generalized void to a 'narrow vast' (92) containing its three shades, finally reduced to three pins and one pinhole (103). Rather than signifying the closure of narrative potential, this arrangement instead describes an image-producing mechanism, the *camera obscura*. This ancient technology in image projection comprises a dark enclosed space and an aperture through which light is admitted, casting an inverted image upon the rear wall or surface (Crary, 1990, 25–66). Both Aristotle (*Problemata*) and Euclid (*Optics*) make reference to the camera obscura, and via medieval Islamic philosophers such as al-Kindi and Alhazen, it passed down to early modern European figures such as Johannes Kepler, who coined the term 'magic lantern', as well as Athanasius Kircher. During the French Revolutionary era, Etienne-Gaspar Robertson used his camera obscura to produce 'elaborate and bizarre spectacles in the crypt of an abandoned Capuchin convent near the Place Vendôme [...] amid ancient tombs and effigies' (Castle, 1988, 36), often drawing on the visual rhetoric of the *memento mori*. Pope had doors installed at each end of his grotto, which he describes, when shut, 'becomes on the instant, from a luminous room, a Camera obscura; on the Walls of which the objects of the river, Hills, Woods, and Boats, are forming a moving Picture in their visible radiations' (Pope, 1956, 296–7). Just as *Worstward Ho* dramatizes the act of creativity and the process of its diminution in a submerged and narrowing space of darkening light, Pope's grotto becomes his own 'personal embodiment of the human mind' (Deutsch, 1996, 116), staging 'a streamlined account of intellection for the reflexive consumption of the eye' (Silver, 2015, 87).

Pope's camera obscura was designed for seclusion, but it also reflected philosophical themes of his day that resonate with the combination of 'grot' and the creating mind in *Worstward Ho*. The camera obscura was commonly used as a metaphor of human cognition in seventeenth-century epistemology (Schmal, 2015, 69–70), from Descartes and Malebranche to its most prominent deployment by John Locke in Book 2 of his *Essay Concerning Human Understanding*: 'the understanding is not much unlike a closet wholly shut from light, with only some little openings left, to let in external visible resemblances, or ideas of things without' (Locke, 1975, 162–3). Locke's project was to establish an epistemology independent of innate ideas, where the mind is a 'white paper' on which impressions are scored. Perception thus transfers images to the mind, and 'thinking was a matter of an internal eye consulting its store; henceforth, thinking could be imagined as the mind ranging over its perceptions' (Silver, 2015, 60). *Worstward Ho* brings about a 'mind' or 'soft' in the course of writing, its 'no dome' denied a facility for producing innate ideas, reduced to 'temple to temple alone' (96). The eye and mind are still able to produce images, despite the aspiration to deplete them towards extinction, and they finally create the pinhole into 'dimmost dim' (103), a camera obscura within which an entire theatre of possibility emerges.

In the late seventeenth century Robert Hooke designed a portable camera obscura to facilitate accurate visual representations of nature. A white screen separated the aperture from the viewer, and thus nature from the artist: 'nature is in this sense not what is visible on the screen; it is what is behind it – the design of things in the absence of design – and it is for this reason that nature, personified, is often represented as though it were behind a veil, curtain, or screen' (Silver, 2015, 65). The pinhole in the penultimate paragraph of *Worstward Ho* embodies Beckett's lifelong aesthetics of impoverishment as an analogous design on nature. The pinhole is the 'meremost minimum' opening to the 'something or nothing behind' the page (*D* 172). It becomes a metaphor of the designer draughting a cosmos, gesturing towards potential new worlds of literary creativity, the geological and philological rift that establishes the possibility for art. The camera obscura concluding *Worstward Ho* both images and imagines all that has come before in Beckett's oeuvre and in literary history. But more than this, in a fitting epic gesture in miniature it induces the reader to imagine all that might still be conceivable in art.

Conclusion – The Masonry of Representation

Worstward Ho presents the reader with one of Beckett's most gnomic and puzzling images: 'There in the sunken head the sunken head' (87). This phrase, a stand-alone sentence, defies the call of representation. Instead the single image of the 'sunken head' is subject to a recursive relation. This compound image captures an essential part of Beckett's lifelong aesthetics: that imperative to express without the various means, powers, desire, vehicle, or matter to express (*D* 139). But it also represents a late moment of clarity, where numerous attempts to view the single consciousness from an external point of view – evident *inter alia* in *Molloy, The Unnamable, Ohio Impromptu*, and particularly *Company* and *Ill Seen Ill Said* – is returned to the location of consciousness, the base matter of the head sunk in its own contemplation. The first mention of the head in *Worstward Ho* arises during the process of composing the first narrative 'subject': 'Head sunk on crippled hands' (83). This image resides in more familiar territory, citing Beckett's own advancing Dupuytren's Contracture, and describing the physical arrangement of head in hands. Andrew Renton traces the emergence of this figure as an 'all-seeing, all-hearing constant' or 'shade' in the manuscript drafts that was to suggest itself as a kind of authorial proxy (Renton, 1992, 108). When the reflexive phrase is added, the text moves from description to something more properly metaphorical: 'the sunken head, given over to thoughts of its own consciousness, rests within its own intellectual purview'. But if the reader were to take the sentence at its literal word, a different kind of image is expressed: the sunken head (consciousness) declines, unable to struggle from its base matter, the 'ring of bone'; or turned another way, the sunken head, as physical object or effigy, is the true location of consciousness and its grandiose gestures of metaphysical liberty, imagination, fancy, and the rest.

Beckett's image gets to the heart of his geological imagination. The sunken head is a kind of statue: matter to be unearthed in an archaeological excavation like the coffer in *Ill Seen Ill Said*, or the 'fossils' in Beckett's intertextual citations, or the geological strata of the mind including its unconscious. Like the Memnon pose it bears a complex genealogy, inferring a history of sculpture and its wordless power to induce narratives and to produce a chain of associated images in a history of textual production. Michel Serres touches on this aetiological function of statuary, at once burying and unearthing the rich histories of language:

> Statues precede languages, these latter having buried them, just as the religions of the word destroy, with blows of stones and letters, the idolatries that engendered them: the second foundation digs beyond or on the nether side of the first, even before the logos would appear. [. . .] Our ideas come to us from idols, language itself admits it; better, our ideas come back from them, like ghosts. (Serres, 2015, 23)

Nohow On returns to some of Beckett's earliest preoccupations, not least the trailing revenants of the living: Belacqua's shade in *More Pricks Than Kicks* and *Echo's Bones* disperses into the shades of Beckett's characters across his novels, ceding ground to the father's shade in *Company*, who abides behind the auditor's right shoulder (14). As the shade departs, so do the 'footfalls' (23), a proxy for Beckett's endogamous intertextuality. What remains is the stone object standing in the place of representation, or the human effigy standing as though made of stone, evident in both *Ill Seen Ill Said* and *Worstward Ho*.

Whilst Beckett's narrators and narrative subjects play out visions of stasis, proximate to effigies, statuary, and gravestone markers, his narratives are also marked by a compulsion to motion and wandering. The auditor in *Company* lies supine in a dark space but is regaled with stories of tramping across the terrain of hillsides and roadways. At one point he is told of standing on a strand, leaning on a staff, 'back to the wash' (35) – a gnomon (γνώμων, 'one that knows') or *cippus* (a low pillar used as gravestone or milestone) measuring out presence until darkness overtakes the moonless scene. Similarly in the first section of the late prose fragment 'The Way' – composed in May 1981, only months before *Worstward Ho* – the unnamed figure traces out a way 'from foot to top and thence on down another way' in pursuit of 'the extremes the will set free' (*TFN* 125). This moving effigy recalls a Christological figure treading a *via dolorosa* – 'Thorns hemmed the way' (125). But rather than spiritual transcendence, a Heraclitean intimacy with the earth prevails via John Burnet's *Greek Philosophy*: 'The way up and the way down [are] one and the same [...] Fire, water, earth is the way down, and earth, water, fire is the way up. And these two ways are forever being traversed in opposite directions at once' (quoted in *C* xi). There is '[l]oose sand underfoot' and 'no sign of remains no sign that none before' (125). The earth underfoot is free from archaeological traces or evidence of prior footfall. The second section of 'The Way' turns the heading '8' on its side into '∞', the lemniscate figure for infinity, as the terrain shifts from one of scaling altitude to moving '[f]orth and back across a barren same winding one-way way' (125). Again it is '[a]s if the earth at rest' and the figure moves at the same pace in the same 'countless time' (126). Each end of the journey is now 'groundless', the fixed 'beaten ways' as though looking upon 'unending void' (126). This turn to the vocabulary of *Worstward Ho* signifies the complex dialectic between the absence of terrain and its singularity. Again there is 'no sign of remains a sign that none before', suggesting the futility of pursuing any evidence of intertext, fossil, remnant statuary, or gravesite – but a final gesture of the immovable actuality of the earth and its constituent mineral facticity is captured in the declaration: 'Bedrock underfoot' (126). The soil and subsoil of narrative is stripped away to reveal the *rockhead* – the geological term for the bedrock's surface – making of the earth underfoot an effigy, an inhuman statue from which narrative generates. This identification with the earth transforms it into a kind of extended mind: a condition where 'mental processes are physically realized in part by structures or processes in our environment' (Slaby, 2014, 32). The narrative worlds of *Nohow On* approach an inhuman or posthuman condition, yet they persistently speak to how the earth yields its material and becomes custodian to the statuary humans extract from and return to it.

> Menhir, dolmen, cromlech, cairn, pyramid, tombstones, boxes for the dead imitating my mother the Earth, mute objects, raised statues, or standing ghosts, resurrected from the black box when the shutter falls down that we thought we had closed for ever, cippi, effigies of marble, granite or plaster, bronze, steel, aluminium, composite materials, full, dense, heavy, immobile, masses marking places and indifferent to time, pierced, bored, hollow, become boxes again, empty, light, white, mobile, automobile engines indifferent to places wandering through time, carrying the living. (Serres, 2015, 24)

Beckett's geological imagination both composes and unearths his texts, installing and revealing in them the remnant substrates of literary endeavour and human consciousness, beginning with his own.

Abbreviations

References throughout are given in the form of parenthetic abbreviations and page numbers keyed to volumes in the Faber & Faber Samuel Beckett series as follows:

ATF   *All That Fall and Other Plays for Radio and Screen*, pref. by Everett Frost, London: Faber & Faber, 2009.

C   *Company*, in *Company, Ill Seen Ill Said, Worstward Ho, Stirrings Still*, ed. Dirk Van Hulle, London: Faber & Faber, 2009.

CP   *The Collected Poems of Samuel Beckett: A Critical Edition*, ed. Seán Lawlor and John Pilling, London: Faber and Faber, 2012.

CSP   *The Complete Short Prose, 1929–1989*, ed. and intro. S. E. Gontarski, New York: Grove, 1995.

D   *Disjecta: Miscellaneous Writings and a Dramatic Fragment*, ed. Ruby Cohn, New York: Grove, 1984.

DF   *Dream of Fair to Middling Women,* ed. Eoin O'Brien and Edith Fournier, New York: Arcade, 2012.

E   *Endgame*, pref. Rónán McDonald, London: Faber & Faber, 2009.

EB   *Echo's Bones*, ed. Mark Nixon, London: Faber & Faber, 2014.

EX   *The Expelled*, in *The Expelled, The Calmative, The End, and First Love*, ed. Christopher Ricks, London: Faber & Faber, 2009.

G   *Waiting for Godot*, pref. Mary Bryden, London: Faber & Faber, 2010.

H   *How It Is*, ed. Édouard Magessa O'Reilly, London: Faber & Faber, 2009.

I   *Ill Seen Ill Said*, in *Company, Ill Seen Ill Said, Worstward Ho, Stirrings Still*, ed. Dirk Van Hulle, London: Faber & Faber, 2009.

K   *Krapp's Last Tape and Other Shorter Plays*, pref. S. E. Gontarski, London: Faber & Faber, 2009.

L1   *The Letters of Samuel Beckett, Volume 1: 1929–1940*, ed. Martha Dow Fehsenfeld and Lois More Overbeck, Cambridge: Cambridge University Press, 2009.

LII   *The Letters of Samuel Beckett, Volume II: 1945–1956*, ed. Martha Dow Fehsenfeld and Lois More Overbeck, Cambridge: Cambridge University Press, 2011.

LIV   *The Letters of Samuel Beckett: Volume IV, 1966–1989*, ed. Martha Dow Fehsenfeld and Lois More Overbeck, Cambridge: Cambridge University Press, 2016.

MD   *Malone Dies*, ed. Peter Boxall, London: Faber & Faber, 2010.

MY   *Molloy*, ed. Shane Weller, London: Faber & Faber, 2009.

MP   *More Pricks Than Kicks*, ed. Cassandra Nelson, London: Faber & Faber, 2010.

M   *Murphy*, ed. and pref. J. C. C. Mays, London: Faber & Faber, 2009.

P   *Proust and Three Dialogues with Georges Duthuit*, London: Calder, 1999.

S   *Stirrings Still*, in *Company, Ill Seen Ill Said, Worstward Ho, Stirrings Still*, ed. Dirk Van Hulle, London: Faber & Faber, 2009.

TC   *The Calmative*, in *The Expelled, The Calmative, The End, and First Love*, ed. Christopher Ricks, London: Faber & Faber, 2009.

TE   *The End*, in *The Expelled, The Calmative, The End, and First Love*, ed. Christopher Ricks, London: Faber & Faber, 2009.

TFN   *Texts for Nothing and Other Shorter Prose, 1950–1976*, ed. Mark Nixon, London: Faber & Faber, 2010.

W   *Watt*, ed. C. J. Ackerley, London: Faber & Faber, 2009.

WH   *Worstward Ho*, in *Company, Ill Seen Ill Said, Worstward Ho, Stirrings Still*, ed. Dirk Van Hulle, London: Faber & Faber, 2009.

U   *The Unnamable*, ed. Steven Connor, London: Faber & Faber, 2010.

Bibliography

Works by Samuel Beckett

All That Fall and Other Plays for Radio and Screen, pref. by Everett Frost, London: Faber & Faber, 2009.

Aufs Schlimmste zu, trans. Erika Tophoven, Frankfurt-am-main: Suhrkamp, 1989.

Beckett's Dream *Notebook*, ed. and intro. John Pilling, Reading: Beckett International Foundation, 1999.

Cap au pire, trans. Edith Fournier, Paris: Éditions de Minuit, 1991.

The Collected Poems of Samuel Beckett: A Critical Edition, ed. Seán Lawlor and John Pilling, London: Faber and Faber, 2012.

Company, Ill Seen Ill Said, Worstward Ho, Stirrings Still, ed. Dirk Van Hulle, London: Faber & Faber, 2009.

The Complete Short Prose, 1929–1989, ed. and intro. S. E. Gontarski, New York: Grove, 1995.

Disjecta: Miscellaneous Writings and a Dramatic Fragment, ed. Ruby Cohn, New York: Grove, 1984.

Dream of Fair to Middling Women, ed. Eoin O'Brien and Edith Fournier, New York: Arcade, 2012.

Echo's Bones, ed. Mark Nixon, London: Faber & Faber, 2014.

Endgame, pref. Rónán McDonald, London: Faber & Faber, 2009.

The Expelled, The Calmative, The End, and First Love, ed. Christopher Ricks, London: Faber & Faber, 2009.

How It Is, ed. Édouard Magessa O'Reilly, London: Faber & Faber, 2009.

Iza saiaku no hō e, trans. Nagashima Kaku, Tokyo: Shoshi-Yamada, 1999.

Krapp's Last Tape and Other Shorter Plays, pref. S. E. Gontarski, London: Faber & Faber, 2009.

Letter to Kay Boyle, 16 December 1983, Box 8, Folder 6, Samuel Beckett Collection, Harry Ransom Humanities Research Center, University of Texas at Austin.

The Letters of Samuel Beckett, Volume 1: 1929–1940, ed. Martha Dow Fehsenfeld and Lois More Overbeck, Cambridge: Cambridge University Press, 2009.

The Letters of Samuel Beckett, Volume II: 1945–1956, ed. Martha Dow Fehsenfeld and Lois More Overbeck, Cambridge: Cambridge University Press, 2011.

The Letters of Samuel Beckett: Volume IV, 1966–1989, ed. Martha Dow Fehsenfeld and Lois More Overbeck, Cambridge: Cambridge University Press, 2016.

'Long Observation of the Ray', RUL MS 2909, Beckett International Foundation Archives, University of Reading.

Malone Dies, ed. Peter Boxall, London: Faber & Faber, 2010.

Molloy, ed. Shane Weller, London: Faber & Faber, 2009.

More Pricks Than Kicks, ed. Cassandra Nelson, London: Faber & Faber, 2010.

Murphy, ed. and pref. J. C. C. Mays, London: Faber & Faber, 2009.

Proust and Three Dialogues with Georges Duthuit, London: Calder, 1999.

Selected Poems 1930–1989, ed. David Wheatley, London: Faber & Faber, 2009.

Sottisier Notebook, MS 2901, Beckett International Foundation Archives, University of Reading.

Texts for Nothing and Other Shorter Prose, 1950–1976, ed. Mark Nixon, London: Faber & Faber, 2010.

The Unnamable, ed. Steven Connor, London: Faber & Faber, 2010.

Waiting for Godot, pref. Mary Bryden, London: Faber & Faber, 2010.

Watt, ed. C. J. Ackerley, London: Faber & Faber, 2009.

Watt [6 notebooks], The Harry Ransom Humanities Research Center, The University of Texas at Austin.

Whoroscope Notebook, RUL MS 3000, Beckett International Foundation Archives, University of Reading.

Worstward Ho [2 manuscripts, 2 typescripts], RUL MS 2602, Beckett International Foundation Archives, University of Reading.

General Bibliography

Abbott, H. Porter (1996), *Beckett Writing Beckett: The Author in the Autograph*, Ithaca and London: Cornell University Press.

Ackerley, C. J. (1993), 'Fatigue and Disgust: The Addenda to *Watt*', in Marius Buning and Lois Oppenheim (ed.), *Samuel Beckett in the 1990s, Samuel Beckett Today/Aujourd'hui*, vol. 2, pp. 175–88.

Ackerley, C. J. (2004), 'Samuel Beckett and the Geology of the Imagination: Toward an Excavation of *Watt*', *Journal of Beckett Studies*, *13*:2, pp. 150–63.

Ackerley, C J. (2005), *Obscure Locks, Simple Keys: The Annotated Watt*, Tallahassee: Journal of Beckett Studies Books.

Ackerley, C. J., and S. E. Gontarski (2004), *The Grove Companion to Samuel Beckett*, New York: Grove.

Balmori, Diana (1991), 'Architecture, Landscape, and the Intermediate Structure: Eighteenth-Century Experiments in Mediation', *Journal of the Society of Architectural Historians*, 50:1, pp. 38–56.

Barry, Elizabeth (2008), 'One's Own Company: Agency, Identity and the Middle Voice in the Work of Samuel Beckett', *Journal of Modern Literature*, 31:2, pp. 115–32.

Bates, Julie (2017), *Beckett's Art of Salvage: Writing and Material Imagination, 1932–1987*, Cambridge: Cambridge University Press.

Benjamin, Walter (1999), *The Arcades Project*, trans. Howard Eiland and Kevin McLaughlin, Cambridge, MA: Harvard University Press.

Bennett, Jane (2010), *Vibrant Matter: A Political Ecology of Things*, Durham, NC and London: Duke University Press.

Blackwell, Mark, ed. (2014), *The Secret Life of Things: Animals, Objects, and It-Narratives in Eighteenth-Century England*, Lewisburg, PA: Bucknell University Press.

Boersma, Gerald P. (2016), *Augustine's Early Theology of Image: A Study in the Development of Pro-Nicene Theology*, New York: Oxford University Press.

Bogost, Ian (2012), *Alien Phenomenology, or What It's Like to Be a Thing*, Minneapolis: University of Minnesota Press.

Bonwick, James [1864] (1986), *Irish Druids and Old Irish Religions*, New York: Dorset.

Boulter, Jonathan (2019), *Posthuman Space in Samuel Beckett's Short Prose*, Edinburgh: Edinburgh University Press.

Boxall, Peter (2009), *Since Beckett: Contemporary Writing in the Wake of Modernism*, London: Continuum.

Braidotti, Rosa (2013), *The Posthuman*, London: Polity.

Brater, Enoch (1983), 'The *Company* Beckett Keeps: The Shape of Memory and One Fablist's Decay of Lying', in Morris Beja, S. E. Gontarski, and Pierre Astier (ed.), *Samuel Beckett: Humanistic Perspectives*, Columbus: Ohio State University Press, pp. 157–71.

Brater, Enoch (1994), *The Drama in the Text: Beckett's Late Fiction*, New York and Oxford: Oxford University Press.

Brown, Bill (1997), *The Material Unconscious: American Amusement, Stephen Crane, and the Economics of Play*, Cambridge, MA: Harvard University Press.

Brown, Bill (2003), *A Sense of Things: The Object Matter of American Literature*, Chicago and London: Chicago University Press.

Brown, Bill (2016), *Other Things*, Chicago: University of Chicago Press.

Brown, Llewellyn (2016), *Beckett, Lacan, and the Voice*, Samuel Beckett in Company, vol. 1, Stuttgart: ibidem.

Browne, Thomas (2014), *Selected Writings*, ed. Kevin Killeen, Oxford: Oxford University Press.

Byron, Mark (2014), 'Modernist Wheelmen', in Rónán McDonald, Julian Murphet, and Sascha Morrell (ed.), *Flann O'Brien and Modernism*, London: Bloomsbury, pp. 213–32.

Byron, Mark (2017), 'Mind, Brain, and Text: Immanent Thinking in *Worstward Ho*', in Arka Chattopadhyay (ed.), *Endlessness of Ending: Samuel Beckett and Extensions of the Mind/Samuel Beckett et les extensions de l'esprit, Samuel Beckett Today/Aujourd'hui*, vol. 29, pp. 126–37.

Campbell, Julie (2001), '"Echo's Bones" and Beckett's Disembodied Voices', in Angela Moorjani and Carola Veit (ed.), *Samuel Beckett: Endlessness in the Year 2000/Samuel Beckett: Fin sans fin en l'an 2000, Samuel Beckett Today/ Aujourd'hui*, vol. 11, pp. 454–60.

Carville, Conor (2018), *Samuel Beckett and the Visual*, Cambridge: Cambridge University Press.

Caselli, Daniella (2005), *Beckett's Dantes: Intertextuality in the Fiction and Criticism*, Manchester: Manchester University Press.

Castle, Terry (1988), 'Phantasmagoria: Spectral Technology and the Metaphorics of Modern Reverie', *Critical Inquiry*, 15:1, pp. 26–61.

Chattopadhyay, Arka (2012), '"Worst in Need of Worse": *King Lear, Worstward Ho* and the Trajectory of Worsening', in Angela Moorjani, Danièle de Ruyter, Dúnlaith Bird, and Sjef Houppermans (ed.), *Early Modern Beckett/Beckett et le début de l'ère moderne, Samuel Beckett Today/Aujourd'hui*, vol. 24, pp. 73–88.

Clark, Andy, and David Chalmers (1998), 'The Extended Mind', *Analysis*, 58:1, pp. 7–19.

Cohen, Jeffrey Jerome (2015), *Stone: An Ecology of the Inhuman*, Minneapolis: University of Minnesota Press.

Coleridge, Samuel Taylor [1816] (1985), 'Kubla Khan', in *Samuel Taylor Coleridge: The Oxford Authors*, ed. H. J. Jackson, Oxford and New York: Oxford University Press, pp. 102–4.

Connor, Steven (2014), *Beckett, Modernism, and the Material Imagination*, Cambridge: Cambridge University Press.

Coole, Diana, and Samantha Frost, eds. (2010), *New Materialisms: Ontology, Agency, and Politics*, Durham, NC: Duke University Press.

Cooley, Jeffrey L. (2008), '*Inana and Šukaletuda*: A Sumerian Astral Myth', *KASKAL: Rivista di storia, ambienti e culture del Vicino Oriente Antico*, 5, pp. 161–72.

Crary, Jonathan (1990), *Techniques of the Observer: On Vision and Modernity in the Nineteenth Century*, Cambridge, MA and London: Massachusetts Institute of Technology Press.

de Wilde, Marc (2012), 'The Dictator's Trust: Regulating and Constraining Emergency Powers in the Roman Republic', *History of Political Thought*, 33:4, pp. 555–77.

Deep Carbon Observatory (10 December 2018), 'Life in Deep Earth Totals 15 to 23 Billion Tonnes of Carbon—Hundreds of Times More than Humans', at https://deepcarbon.net/life-deep-earth-totals-15-23-billion-tonnes-carbon.

Deutsch, Helen (1996), *Resemblance and Disgrace: Alexander Pope and the Deformation of Culture*, Cambridge, MA: Harvard University Press.

Dukes, Gerry (1993), 'Quarrying the Trilogy', in Marius Buning and Lois Oppenheim (ed.), *Samuel Beckett in the 1990s, Samuel Beckett Today/ Aujourd'hui*, vol. 2, pp. 197–204.

Dukes, Hunter (2016), 'Samuel Beckett and the Fantasy of Lithic Preservation', *Irish Studies Review*, 25:1, pp. 24–41.

Eliade, Mircea (1996), *Patterns in Comparative Religion*, trans. Rosemary Sheed, Lincoln and London: University of Nebraska Press.

Eliot, T. S. (2015), *The Poems of T. S. Eliot, Volume I: Collected and Uncollected Poems*, ed. Christopher Ricks and Jim McCue, London: Faber & Faber.

Feldman, Matthew (2006), *Beckett's Books: A Cultural History of Samuel Beckett's 'Interwar Notes'*, London: Continuum.

Finegan, Jack (1992), *The Archaeology of the New Testament: The Life of Jesus and the Beginning of the Early Church*, rev. ed., Princeton: Princeton University Press.

Freud, Sigmund [1896] (1962), 'The Aetiology of Hysteria', in *Early Psycho-Analytic Publications*, vol. 3 of *The Standard Edition of the Complete Psychological Works of Sigmund Freud*, ed. and trans. James Strachey with Anna Freud, Alix Strachey, and Alan Tyson, London: Hogarth Press and The Institute of Psycho-Analysis, pp. 187–221.

Gordon, Benjamin D. (2019), 'Archaeology of the Postexilic Period and the Writings', in *The Oxford Handbook of the Writings of the Hebrew Bible*, ed. Donn F. Morgan, Oxford: Oxford University Press, pp. 49–63.

Grusin, Richard, ed. (2015), *The Nonhuman Turn*, Minneapolis: University of Minnesota Press.

Hake, Sabine (1993) '*Saxa Loquuntur*: Freud's Archaeology of the Text', *boundary 2*, 20:1, pp. 147–73.

Hamilton, Scott Eric (2018), 'Antiquarianism, Archaeology, and Aporetic Immanence in Beckett's Prose', *Irish Studies Review*, 26:2, pp. 163–80.

Harmon, Graham (2002), *Tool-Being: Heidegger and the Metaphysics of Objects*, Chicago: Open Court.

Harrison, Robert Pogue (2003), *The Dominion of the Dead*, Chicago: University of Chicago Press.

Haslam, Molly C. (2012), *A Constructive Theology of Intellectual Disability: Human Being as Mutuality and Response*, New York: Fordham University Press.

Heidegger, Martin [1950] (1993), 'The Origin of the Work of Art', in *Basic Writings*, ed. David Farrell Krell, London: Routledge, pp. 143–212.

Herity, Michael (1974), *Irish Passage Graves: Neolithic Tomb Builders in Ireland and Britain, 2500 BC*, Dublin: Irish University Press.

Hisgen, Ruud (1998), *The Silencing of the Sphinx*, vol. 2, Leiden: Private Edition.

Hunkeler, Thomas (1997), *Echos de l'ego dans l'oeuvre de Samuel Beckett*, Paris: L'Harmattan.

Illich, Ivan (1993), *In the Vineyard of the Text: A Commentary to Hugh's Didascalicon*, Chicago: University of Chicago Press.

Ingold, Tim (1993), 'The Temporality of the Landscape', *World Archaeology*, 25:2, pp. 152–74.

Jeans, James (1929), *The Universe Around Us*, Cambridge: Cambridge University Press.

Keatinge, Benjamin (2007), '"The Hammers of the Stone-Cutters": Samuel Beckett's Stone Imagery', *Irish University Review*, 37:3, pp. 322–39.

Knowlson, James (1972), *Light and Darkness in the Theatre of Samuel Beckett*, London: Turret.

Knowlson, James (1983), 'Beckett's Bits of Pipe', in Morris Beja, S. E. Gontarski, and Pierre Astier (ed.), *Samuel Beckett: Humanistic Perspectives*, Columbus: Ohio State University Press, pp. 16–25.

Knowlson, James (1996), *Damned to Fame: The Life of Samuel Beckett*, London: Bloomsbury.

Krance, Charles (1993), *Company/Compagnie and A Piece of Monologue/Solo: A Bilingual Variorum Edition*, New York: Garland.

Krance, Charles (1996), *Samuel Beckett's Mal vu mal dit/Ill Seen Ill Said: A Bilingual, Evolutionary, and Synoptic Variorum Edition*, New York and London: Garland.

Langlois, Christopher (2017), *Samuel Beckett and the Terror of Literature*, Edinburgh: Edinburgh University Press.

Liddell, Henry George, and Robert Scott (1940), *A Greek-English Lexicon*, rev. ed., ed. Henry Stuart Jones, Oxford: Clarendon.

Locke, John [1689] (1975), *An Essay Concerning Human Understanding*, ed. Peter H. Nidditch, Oxford: Clarendon.

Long, Joseph (2000), 'Divine Intertextuality: Samuel Beckett, *Company, Le Dépeupleur*', in Mary Bryden and Lance St John Butler (ed.), *Beckett and Religion/Beckett et la religion, Samuel Beckett Today/Aujourd'hui*, vol. 10, pp. 145–58.

Long, Priscilla (2016), *Fire and Stone: Where Do We Come From? What Are We? Where Are We Going?*, Athens: University of Georgia Press.

Moretti, Franco (2013), *Distant Reading*, London: Verso.

Mori, Naoya (2008), 'Becoming Stone: A Leibnizian Reading of Beckett's Fiction', in Minako Okamuro, Naoya Mori, Bruno Clément, Sjef Houppermans, Angela Moorjani, and Anthony Uhlmann (ed.), *Borderless Beckett/Beckett sans frontiers, Samuel Beckett Today/Aujourd'hui*, vol. 19, pp. 201–10.

Mosshammer, Alden A. (2008), *The Easter Computus and the Origins of the Christian Era*, Oxford: Oxford University Press.

Napolin, Julie Beth (2017), 'Elliptical Sound: Audibility and the Space of Reading', in Julian Murphet, Helen Groth, and Penelope Hone (ed.), *Sounding Modernism: Rhythm and Sonic Mediation in Modern Literature and Film*, Edinburgh: Edinburgh University Press, pp. 109–29.

Nixon, Mark (2006), '"Guess Where": From Reading to Writing in Beckett', *Genetic Joyce Studies*, 6, www.antwerpjamesjoycecenter.com/GJS6/GJS6Nixon.htm.

O'Brien, Eoin (1986), *The Beckett Country*, Dublin: Black Cat; London: Faber.

O'Donoghue, Diane (2019), *On Dangerous Ground: Freud's Visual Cultures of the Unconscious*, London: Bloomsbury.

O'Reilly, Edouard Magessa (2001), *Samuel Beckett's Comment c'est/How It Is and/et L'image: A Critical Genetic Edition/Une edition critique-génétique*, New York and London: Routledge.

Olivier, Laurent (2001), 'Duration, Memory, and the Nature of the Archaeological Record', in Håkan Karlsson (ed.), *It's About Time: The Concept of Time in Archaeology*, Gothenburg: Bricoleur Press, pp. 61–70.

Olsen, Bjørrnar (2010), *In Defense of Things: Archaeology and the Ontology of Objects*, Lanham, MD: AltaMira Press.

Olsen, Bjørrnar, Michael Shanks, Timothy Webmore, and Christopher Witmore (2012), *Archaeology: The Discipline of Things*, Berkeley and Los Angeles: University of California Press.

Parsons, Cóilín (2013), 'The Turd in the Rath: Antiquarians, the Ordnance Survey, and Beckett's Irish Landscape', *Journal of Beckett Studies*, 22:1, pp. 83–107.

Perloff, Marjorie (1990), *Poetic License: Essays on Modernist and Postmodernist Lyric*, Evanston, IL: Northwestern University Press.

Pilling, John (1982), '*Company*', *Journal of Beckett Studies*, 7, pp. 127–31.

Pilling, John (1986), '"Nohow On": *Worstward Ho*', in *Beckett at Eighty: A Celebration*, ed. James Knowlson, Reading: The Beckett Archive of Reading University, pp. 25–6.

Pilling, John (2005), 'Dates and Difficulties in Beckett's *Whoroscope Notebook*', in Dirk Van Hulle (ed.), *Beckett the European*, Tallahassee: Journal of Beckett Studies Books, pp. 39–48.

Pilling, John (2006), *A Samuel Beckett Chronology*, Houndmills: Palgrave.

Pope, Alexander (1956), *The Correspondence of Alexander Pope*, ed. George Sherburn, 5 vols., Oxford: Oxford University Press.

Potkay, Adam (2007), *The Story of Joy: From the Bible to Late Romanticism*, Cambridge: Cambridge University Press.

Price, Alexander (2014), 'Beckett's Bedrooms: On Dirty Things and Thing Theory', *Journal of Beckett Studies*, 23:2, pp. 155–77.

Rabaté, Jean-Michel (2016), 'The Posthuman, or the Humility of the Earth', in *Think Pig!: Beckett at the Limits of the Human*, New York: Fordham University Press, pp. 37–48.

Renton, Andrew (1992), '*Worstward Ho* and the End(s) of Representation', in John Pilling and Mary Bryden (ed.), *The Ideal Core of the Onion: Reading Beckett Archives*, Reading: Beckett International Foundation, pp. 99–135.

Rodriguez, Michael Angelo (2004), '"Everywhere Stone is Gaining": The Struggle for the Sacred in Samuel Beckett's *Ill Seen Ill Said*', in Anthony Uhlmann, Sjef Houppermans, and Bruno Clément (ed.), *After Beckett/D'Apres Beckett, Samuel Beckett Today/Aujourd'hui*, vol. 14, pp. 105–16.

Schmal, Dániel (2015), 'Visual Perception and the Cartesian Concept of Mind: Descartes and the *Camera obscura*', in Tamás Demeter, Kathryn Murphy, and Claus Zittel (ed.), *Conflicting Values of Inquiry: Ideologies of Epistemology in Early Modern Europe*, Leiden: Brill, pp. 69–91.

Serle, John (1745), *A Plan of Mr Pope's Grotto: As It was Left at His Death, with a Plan and Perspective View of the Grotto*, London: R. Dodsley.

Serres, Michel (2015), *Statues: The Second Book of Foundations*, trans. Randolph Burks, London: Bloomsbury.

Shaw, Joanne (2012), 'Light and Darkness in Elsheimer, Caravaggio, Rembrandt and Beckett', in Angela Moorjani, Danièle de Ruyter, Dúnlaith Bird, and Sjef Houppermans (ed.), *Early Modern Beckett/Beckett et le début de l'ère moderne, Samuel Beckett Today/Aujourd'hui*, vol. 24, pp. 219–31.

Shaw, Joanne (2013), 'The Figure in the Landscape in Jack Yeats and in Samuel Beckett', in Jürgen Siess, Matthijs Engelberts, and Angela Moorjani (ed.),

Beckett in the Cultural Field/Beckett dans le champ culturel, Samuel Beckett Today/Aujourd'hui, vol. 25, pp. 31–43.

Shelley, P. B. (1977), *Shelley's Poetry and Prose*, ed. Donald H. Reiman and Sharon B. Powers, New York: W. W. Norton.

Silver, Sean (2015), *The Mind Is a Collection: Case Studies in Eighteenth-Century Thought*, Philadelphia: University of Pennsylvania Press.

Slaby, Jan (2014), 'Emotions and the Extended Mind', in Christian von Scheve and Mikko Salmela (ed.), *Collective Emotions*, Oxford: Oxford University Press, pp. 32–46.

Smith, Frederik N. (2002), *Beckett's Eighteenth Century*, Houndmills and New York: Palgrave.

Tilley, Christopher (1994), *A Phenomenology of Landscape*, London: Berg.

Trumbower, Jeffrey A. (2001), *Rescue for the Dead: The Posthumous Salvation of Non-Christians in Early Christianity*, Oxford: Oxford University Press.

Tubridy, Derval (2018), *Samuel Beckett and the Language of Subjectivity*, Cambridge: Cambridge University Press.

Van Hulle, Dirk, and Mark Nixon (2013), *Samuel Beckett's Library*, Cambridge: Cambridge University Press.

Weel, Adriaan van der (1998), *The Silencing of the Sphinx*, vol. 1, Leiden: Private Edition.

Weller, Shane (2005), *A Taste for the Negative: Beckett and Nihilism*, London: Legenda.

Willson, Anthony Beckles (1998), *Alexander Pope's Grotto in Twickenham*, London: Garden History Society and Twickenham Museum.

Wimbush, Andy (2016), 'Paleozoic Profounds: Samuel Beckett and Ecological Time', in Jan Baetens, Sascha Bru, Dirk De Geest, David Martens, Bart Van Den Bossche, and Robin Vogelzang (ed.), *Time and Temporality in Literary Modernism* (1900–1950), Leuven: Peeters, pp. 3–14.

Cambridge Elements☰

Beckett Studies

Dirk Van Hulle
University of Oxford
Dirk Van Hulle is Professor of Bibliography and Modern Book History at the University of Oxford and director of the Centre for Manuscript Genetics at the University of Antwerp.

Mark Nixon
University of Reading
Mark Nixon is Associate Professor in Modern Literature at the University of Reading and the Co-Director of the Beckett International Foundation.

About the Series

This series presents cutting-edge research by distinguished and emerging scholars, providing space for the most relevant debates informing Beckett studies as well as neglected aspects of his work. In times of technological development, religious radicalism, unprecedented migration, gender fluidity, environmental and social crisis, Beckett's works find increased resonance. Elements in Beckett Studies is a key resource for readers interested in the current state of the field.

Elements in the Series

Printed in the United States
By Bookmasters